My Journey to an Organized Life

A Creative Road Map
for Organizing Your
Time, Space, and Finances

KATHERINE TREZISE / JENNIFER POWER

Names, characters, businesses, places, events, and incidences in this book are fictional. They are products of the authors' imaginations. Any resemblance to actual persons, living or dead, or actual events is purely coincidental.

Although the authors and publisher have made every effort to ensure that the information in this book was correct at press time, the authors and publisher do not assume and hereby disclaim any liability to any party for any loss, damage, or disruption caused by errors or omissions, whether such errors or omissions result from negligence, accident, or any other cause.

© 2015 Katherine Trezise and Jennifer Power
All rights reserved. This publication is protected by copyright, and permission must be obtained from the authors prior to any prohibited reproduction, storage in a retrieval system, or transmission in any form or by any means, electronic, mechanical, photocopying, recording, or likewise.

My Personal, Legal, Medical, and Financial Information worksheets © Absolutely Organized, LLC. Used with permission.

Cover design and graphics by: Lisa Guarrera

Library of Congress Control Number: 2015910663
ISBN: 978-1514196267

Published by: CreateSpace
                North Charleston, SC

Ordering information: http://www.amazon.com/dp/1514196263

First Edition
First Printing
2015
Printed in the United States of America

May this story inspire those souls who are desperately searching for a change in their lives yet have lacked the motivation, support, courage, hope, confidence, and knowledge of someone's own personal life experiences to help take them there.

K.T. To Tom, Greg, and Meredith Trezise for their support and encouragement, and in memory of my mother, Edna Hamilton, who gave me my first organizing lessons.

J.P. To Rob, Ryan, and Brady for their love and support on this journey.

TABLE OF CONTENTS

The Eve of a New Millennium — 3

Listening to the Grandfather Clock in a New Way — 7
   Now It's Your Turn
   Planning Your Journey to Freedom from Disorganization — 13
      Should I Get My Life Organized—Or Not? — 13
      My Journey to an Organized Life—Timeline — 14
      Evaluate My Plan—Is It On POINT? — 14

Time to Tango — 17
   Now It's Your Turn
   Freedom from the Unimportant: Organizing Your Time — 23
      My Roles and Responsibilities — 23
      My Weekly Schedule — 25

Cleaning the Monsters Out of the House—Without Sprays — 27

P.S. Keeping it Real and Honest — 31
   Now It's Your Turn
   Freedom from Clutter: Organizing Your Rooms and Storage Areas — 33
      The MESS Formula — 33

Swinging Over the Money Pit—A Rope Please — 37
   Now It's Your Turn
   Freedom from Financial Chaos: Organizing How You Spend Your Money — 47
      My Personal Financial Goals — 47
      Reality Check: The Good, The Bad, and The Ugly — 48
      Identify the Changes in Spending You Will Make — 52
      If Your Expenses Exceed Your Income — 52

TABLE OF CONTENTS

    If You Have Unsecured Debt   52
    Take Steps to Achieve Your Financial Goals   54

The Second Honeymoon   57
    Now It's Your Turn
    Freedom from Paper Piles: Organizing Your Paperwork   65
        WHY do I need to keep this paper?   65
        WHO cares whether or not I keep this paper?   66
        WHAT is the next action I need to do with this paper?   70
        WHEN will I need to find this paper?   70
        WHERE is the best place to store this paper?   70
        Got Electronic Clutter?   74
        What to Shred vs. What to Recycle   74

Mary, Accidents Happen   75
    Now It's Your Turn
    Freedom from the Daily Mail: Organizing Your Bill-Paying Process   81
        The MESS Formula   81
        Electronic Bill-Paying Options   83
        Organizing Your Medical Bills   86

What If . . .   91
    Now It's Your Turn
    Freedom from Worry: Organizing Your Estate Planning   93
        Legal Documents You Need to Have   93
        Last Will and Testament (or Revocable Living Trust)   93
        Power of Attorney   93
        Advance Health Care Directive   94
        Where to Store Your Legal Documents   94

TABLE OF CONTENTS

What My Family Needs to Know 95
How to Create Your What My Family Needs to Know *Booklet* 96

Making a List and Checking it Twice 115
Now It's Your Turn
Freedom from Guilt: Organizing Your Gift Giving 119
Plan and Track Your Charitable Giving 119
Make Your Gift-Giving List, but Check it Twice 119

Ready for Reflections 121
Now It's Your Turn
Celebrating Your Freedom from Disorganization 123

Introduction

With a combined total of 28 years in the professional organizing field, we have seen and read it all. During this time, we have witnessed hundreds of organizing books published. Though there are many beneficial organizing books in print, they all seem to be lacking one thing—a relatable character.

When working with clients, no matter their degree of disorganization, the personal factor, that one-on-one relationship that is forged between the client and the organizer becomes paramount. It is that guiding hand that not only has the know-how to get someone to where they wish to be, but is present for the journey, no matter the struggles, anxiety, fears, or overwhelming thoughts. And it is that guiding hand that reminds you: "You are not the first one to take a walk on the path to organization; the path to organization is well trodden and has been walked by many; the path to organization is easier to navigate with a trusted companion; the path to organization will eventually take you to the end result you desire."

So how did we decide to fill the void and supply a relatable guiding hand that has been lacking in organizing books? We invented Mary. Mary represents the conglomeration of traits we typically see in our clients who are challenged, to a greater or lesser degree, by chronic disorganization. You will note that we purposely do not give a physical description of Mary; she is meant to represent all of us. She does not hoard to any extreme nor does she instantly know how to get to the place she wants to be. Like most people dealing with some form of disorganization, she has moments of triumph, but she also has moments of set-backs and defeat.

We have written Mary's chronicle over one year's time. This is only to allow the reader a sense of measureable time and to provide the story with a set beginning and ending time. For some people who struggle with the negative consequences of chronic disorganization, one year isn't enough—the path to an organized life is a continuous journey of uphill and downhill battles. By using Mary's story, we strive to give readers hope and to show how in just one year's time many organizational goals can be achieved. The important thing to note about Mary is that she is a ready and willing candidate. This is the key. She is ready to make a change even when the change process is difficult, and she is ready to accept the help of others.

We also want to take a moment to explain why we include Mary's family in the story. When someone is trying to organize their life, family can be either a contributing solution or a contributing problem to the process. While some family members are supportive and ready to lend a hand, we often see instances where family members are unwilling to help, have grown frustrated and tired of fighting over a relative's disorganized lifestyle, or have no reason to think that change is possible. Mary usually has the support and backing of her family members, but this isn't always the case. When there are underlying mental health issues contributing to disorganization such as depression, obsessive compulsive disorder, anxiety disorder, attention deficit/hyperactivity disorder, hoarding disorder, or compulsive buying behaviors, a psychotherapist may be needed to assist an individual so they are able to reach their desired organizational goals.

The inclusion of the *Now It's Your Turn* portions after each chapter was designed to give you the *creative* tools to accomplish the same goals Mary sets. Again, this is where *My Journey to an Organized Life* follows a different format. You will begin by setting your goals just like Mary does, on a restaurant café napkin. Epiphanies don't always occur when you think they will. It is okay to be creative. There are many ways to arrive at the same desired destination. We will offer creative fixes to reaching your organizational goals. And throughout your own organizational journey, Mary will be there to support you; after all, she has already been through the process and is meant to be your guiding hand.

Now, we introduce you to Mary . . .

To tell you my story, well, I can tell you it was a long road, no, a journey. I walked a very personal journey. We all walk them. I found the hard part was choosing the right path and sticking to it no matter how hard things became. Like the Robert Frost poem I had read in high school, one day I had to choose to take the road less traveled.

It was the day, just like every day before, when I stumbled to the bathroom to get ready for a New Year's party. Yes, I stumbled. I was well rested, at least I thought I was, but I stumbled on the same pile of laundry that was piled in the hallway. That same pile of clothes that was always there every day, mocking me, reminding me I was stuck, making me feel tired even though I wasn't sleepy. It just laughed. And then I made it to the bathroom and I had to fish for my toothbrush. I wasted more of my precious time fumbling through makeup containers to find the right shade of lip color and eye liner. I had to wear my mask every day.

Again, more time wasted as I looked for clothes to wear that may or may not fit. I was too tired to take the time to care about the monster that lived in my closet. He was the one who messed everything up and refused to get lost—to let me be at peace. It wasn't my fault.

It was that day, that particular moment, that instant in time it started. It was the day I decided I was tired of being laughed at and tired of facing the monsters. It was that day I knew I needed to make a change.

This is the story of my journey. Why am I sharing this with you? To show you there is hope. To let you know you are not alone. To tell you that I was able to find a different road after all the years of feeling isolated and on my own—like no one understood me. The problem . . . I didn't understand myself.

It takes courage to look at yourself, to truly stand in front of a mirror and ask the tough questions. *Who am I? What do I see? Who is it I want to be?* But it takes even more strength to decide to walk another road. To cross over and through sticker bushes, tall grasses, and brush. You know you will inevitably get hurt by thorns, you know you will dirty your clothes, and you know you will have to cut through areas of vegetation that contain areas behind which you can't see. At times it will be scary.

It was hard. I was stuck in many places. But I'm not anymore. I decided to cross over to the other side and take a path I didn't know, the one I didn't quite understand. And now I am a new Mary. We each have to find our own path to follow. What I can tell you is it was worth it. In every way it was worth it. My life, my relationships, my own new-found free time—it was all worth it.

Now, I, Mary, do consider myself responsibly unleashed. Well done, Mary.

My Journey to an Organized Life

THE EVE OF A NEW MILLENNIUM
December 31st, 1999

It was just another day of not being able to do anything right. I guess somewhere along the line I had just come to believe it must be true, that I truly was incapable and useless.

I kicked the basket of what used to be clean laundry aside so I could reach the pull string and turn on the light in my bedroom closet. The sudden brightness of the single bulb in the ceiling fixture awakened the monster that hid inside my closet. It was staring at me, as usual, hiding in the cramped quarters. I spoke to that monster. We had conversations often. *I know I was supposed to find new homes for my too-skinny and too-big-for-me-clothes last summer. That would have given me a little more closet room. But I was busy. Besides, those too-skinny-for-me-clothes were supposed to fit me again by now.*

The exercise bike in the corner of my bedroom rolled its eyes at me. At least I thought it did. It was lonely from non-use. Honestly, I couldn't actually see its eyes because they were draped with my shirts and dresses. I used its arms to temporarily hold some summer clothes I had planned to store in the attic. The clothes had never made it up there.

Downstairs, the grandfather clock chimed six times. My anxiety level went up a notch with each chime. Wait for it, wait for it—his voice, my husband Horace's voice wouldn't be far behind, and there it was. "Would you hurry up, please? What's taking you so long? We're going to be late if we don't leave right now! You knew what time we had to leave. Why do you always wait until the last minute? You had all day to get ready." Many were the times I had partaken in that tango. Horace had family roots in Argentina; he was an expert at the tango. But even the clock couldn't keep beat to the rhythm of his ridiculousness.

I clenched my teeth in pain. A pinched nerve sent a jolt that radiated through my neck and shoulder as I tried to shove the tightly-packed hanging clothes aside. I was looking for my favorite black dress. I love the way I look in that dress. The clothes hangers barely budged. Alas, I found the treasure that I so longed to wear stuck between the un-purged too-skinny clothes. There, lifeless and wrinkled, hung my favorite black dress.

I reached in for it, freeing it from its embrace with the adjoining hangers, and saw a grease stain on the front. Why did that grease stain have to be on my favorite dress? The dress I forgot, of course, to take to the cleaners. Damn it! Oh well, just another item I could shop for, just another thing to add to the credit card bill. I could never do anything right. My cat Fiasco purred as if in agreement with me as he brushed against my leg. How easy life must be for a cat. All I knew was that I had nothing clean that was fit to wear, I was late again, and Horace was ticked-off! Another year was ending just like it began, just like they all have begun for the last umpteen years. Why did I even care?

This was to be the party to end all parties, or at least that is how the new millennium should have rung in. But as I have explained, nothing ever seems to go quite right in my world; the world with me in it; the world of Mary.

You want the story of my life? It would bore you to tears. Just as boring is the story of the eve of that new millennium. It was to be the big New Year's party. The year 2000 was breathing down my neck. The party was just another thing I had added to my to-do list. Horace took to catering to the needs of his financial business companions. Many were also his golf buddies. They were used to getting together. Horace was a member of one of the finest golf clubs in the area. (And he had the nerve to complain about what I spent shopping!) It was always another work party or event. Really, I think I would have preferred to go to sleep that night. I didn't really feel like I had all that much I wanted to celebrate. I wore a stupid blue dress to ring in the new millennium. I would have felt so much more comfortable in the black one. Why was I so brainless? My blue dress was part of my too-big-for-me-collection that the monster still held onto in my closet. I wished I could stop thinking of that monster for just one night, but he seemed to follow me wherever I went. There should be a bug spray for monsters.

Too tired to make simple talk and carry on conversations, and already upset from the bickering I had to endure with Horace in the car on the way to what was just a business function, I found this night was definitely not my idea of a romantic New Year's gala ball. I remember spending part of the evening preparing to run for the hills, to get away, to go somewhere I felt like I belonged. I wanted to just sit down and cry. Why bother? Who would care? But I would cry on what should be a most beautiful and celebrated night. A night of what should be new, clean beginnings. And through my view of the hall window a faint snow started to fall from the sky, the flakes trying their best to cover the green that was left on the wintered lawn. It was clean and white. Clean and white.

And so I sat watching those flakes while I gingerly sipped at a martini offered to me by a thirty-something male member of the catering staff. His hair was just starting to show the maturity of a salt and pepper color mix. I wondered where his wife was this evening—he was to die for! Surely she was luckier than I. I pictured her sitting at home watching a movie and enjoying her children. Perhaps their children were already tucked in bed. It was getting late and she was probably enjoying some alone time. The kind of time you spend in a home when everything has a place and is in the exact place where it belongs. It was surely the kind of home where someone could entertain on New Year's Eve. A home you could invite business partners to, not an over-glorified business staff room in a small hall with tables and chairs. A tranquil place that was so much more than a house with too much stuff: A home. That's where I wanted to go, home—clean and white . . . a home.

People-watcher is how I would best describe the behavior I exhibited when out at an event like this. I hated listening to the stories of those who *had it together*. And with that thought, just like clockwork, just like the chime on Horace's old, inherited grandfather clock at the house, the one that was supposed to keep us on time, on pace, in line, Horace's time, I had a visitor sit down next to me. I dreaded the uninvited visitor. People could be monsters, too. I was trapped. No place to go. Not the small talk again. *Yes, I do believe I know your daughter. Yes, she was very talented the other night in the senior-class holiday play. Yes, my daughter Nadine has heard her name mentioned at school. Yes, I'm sure you're very proud. Johns Hopkins you say? Yes, I'm sure her grades must have been exceedingly good in order to receive a scholarship from such a fine school*. And of course, it went on, and on. It always does. The talks, the closet, the clothes, the bills, and the stuff—all I wanted to do was find home.

Horace and I arrived at the house early the next morning after the party. We were both exhausted because we had to stay and help tie-up loose ends from the event like tipping that nice-to-look-at-thirty-something-waiter and making sure we loaded the car with the leftover food items. The food would prove a big help when I woke up in the morning with my martini hangover, surely still in my silly blue dress. I already knew I would be too exhausted to change. At least my family would have something to eat. Then again, I would be lucky to find room for the food in the refrigerator, or the spare refrigerator in the garage. A monster lived in my refrigerators, too.

Again, I desperately felt the need to have some type of monster removal spray. I had never seen that available for sale in the numerous shopping catalogs the monster kept stashing in my mailbox. The nice people from the TV shopping networks didn't have it in stock, and I would know, as I have a premiere account and place orders on a weekly basis. The UPS man and I are quite good friends, in fact, he knows my garage keypad security code in case it rains. He even brings treats for my cats: Moxie, Glums, and Fiasco.

Horace has threatened to put parental blocks on my television shopping channels. Another way I am to stay in tune with his clock—tick tock, tick tock. Wait until Horace sees the Christmas gift I've given him this year—the new millennium credit card bill! I went somewhat overboard with the Christmas shopping again this year. No significantly huge deal; I always overspend each month. That is another monster that needs to be tamed. Those monsters just seem to hang out everywhere. It's a shame I can't write my credit card bills off as a business expense like Horace's awful New Year's party. And so it goes on, tick tock, tick tock. Maybe I'll grab another martini. Oh, joy to the world!

LISTENING TO THE GRANDFATHER CLOCK IN A NEW WAY
January 1st, 2000

New Year's Day found me out at one of my local haunts, Yanni's Café, for wouldn't you know it was right in the midst of one of my most favorite outlet shopping malls. The New Year brought with it sales aplenty and the chance to come home with a lot more stuff for me, and my monsters, that I knew I didn't need. But it felt so good buying each and every one of those things that now laughed at me in their bags from across the restaurant booth where I found myself sitting, dreaming.

I haven't a clue as to how long the waitress was standing next to my table before I came out of my reverie and heard her ask for my order. Who cares; she could wait. Petite with wavy, velvet black hair, her button front shirt could hardly contain her youthful womanliness. Yes, I remember the days. The tag on her shirt read, *Nikki*. The tag didn't require any neon bulbs to help promote the display.

I already knew what I wanted because it was the same thing I ordered for myself every time I came here. The deluxe bacon burger with cheese fries. The bags of clothing I just purchased rattled and shook, laughing at me again—those little monsters! They knew my recent clothes purchases just barely fit. There was no room for an ounce of weight gain. Honestly, I think the clothing manufacturers forgot how to cut clothes to the proper size. I have never worn a size fourteen IN MY LIFE! No problem, they can laugh. Let Horace laugh when he sees the bill. He is the financial guru. He keeps track of money like he keeps track of time. As I said, nothing in the new millennium was any different, nothing had changed.

When Nikki brought me my drink, a Diet Coke as I prefer to eat and not drink my calories, I found myself absent-mindedly doodling on my napkin. I would say I was a little embarrassed, but then, I think the waitress already thought I was not quite sane so why should I really care? There, doodled on my napkin, were Moxie, Glums, and Fiasco, my cats. I was an art major in college, but I think I did them enough justice for an appearance as stick figures on the back of a paper napkin. Fiasco's golden stripes looked just as crooked and mismatched as ever and Moxie was on my lap, alpha cat, right where he likes to be. What haughtiness he could display. And then poor Glums, skittish little guy in the back of the picture next to the clock. He is deaf so I think he often feels left out and depressed. He is the only one who can stand to sit next to the clock, surely because he can't hear it. And there I was, sitting on a couch, reading the book I bought last Christmas, the one I keep meaning to read. I don't even remember where I put that book. And there was Horace, standing next to Glums and his prized clock, dressed to hit the golf course—he was smiling. He was smiling at *me*! Hold on; back-up just a minute! That can't be me on the couch. But it was me, and I was wearing that new cute bootleg jean and cashmere sweater twinset I just bought at the outlet mall. I looked great! I must finally be using that exercise bike in my room for what it was meant for, exercise, and not as a clothes hanger. And Nadine, my beautiful daughter, was waiting by the front door inviting her school friends into the house. Well, what about that!

"Nikki," I said as she still stood there staring at me, "I have always thought about ordering one of your Yanni's Greek Signature Salads. If it isn't too late, I would like to change my order."

"Sure." She looked at me as if I was beyond PMS, which I was, and I took comfort in knowing her turn was coming one day. "I'll put that in."

As I sat and ate my salad, I found I was doodling again on the napkin. Me on my exercise bike, and I must further accentuate it was a *skinny* figure of me on my exercise bike, with a little cleavage thrown in to add some artistic worth. In order to ride the bike my clothes that needed to be put away, stored, or laundered were totally out of the picture. My house looked like a home. And as I enjoyed drawing, daydreaming, and my yummy Greek salad, I realized that what I was drawing wasn't totally unobtainable. I mean, Horace was smiling and I looked really good. And besides, the bags across the booth were no longer laughing. The monsters were quieting down.

I quickly took the napkin while I was in the mood and thought about the changes I would love to make this new millennium. Maybe it would be possible. Here is a copy of my napkin.

After lunch when I arrived home, I sat down at my work desk. Good grief, the paper piles were everywhere! Oh my, so this is where I left most of my scrapbooking supplies. I love to scrapbook but haven't had the time to do it—for years! It took me awhile to shovel down through all the stuff that had accumulated on my desk so I could get to my laptop, but it was worth it. I made-up my own little list of things I would like to do to ring in the new millennium. I knew I couldn't do them all at once, but anything was better than what I was doing now—nothing.

This was my initial plan:

My Journey to an Organized Life—Timeline

My Destinations (the end results I want):	Start On:	Complete By:
Have a system to get control over how I spend my time	January 1	January 2
A kitchen that contains only the stuff we actually use, and that stuff will be organized so we can actually find and use it	January 25	February 14
A garage we can park our cars in	Not now—wait until summer	Not now—wait until summer
Understand how we're spending our money and have a spending & savings plan for this year	February 15	February 28
An organized paperwork system that contains only what we really need to keep	March 1	March 31

I sat there for a moment and stared at what I had created. The papers I just cleared away still laughed, but they were contained in just one spot on my desk and I could use my laptop. Who was laughing now! I couldn't believe it. What madness had I started? What would the monsters have to say? What would Horace and Nadine have to say? Would Horace really start smiling at me? Would Nadine, in her senior year of high school, finally feel comfortable inviting friends over? It was time to make some changes for me, Mary. And as I sat and thought about my new lists I felt a little bit hopeful. I saw those doodles on my napkins as a possibility, a real possibility and not just a dream.

If Glums could stand being near that awful old clock, I guess I could put on deaf ears and stand next to it, too. But maybe that was part of my problem all along. I was remembering that tick tock right then and it didn't sound so bad. In fact, it reminded me of Horace and that wasn't so bad at all.

Moxie walked right across my computer keyboard and jumped onto my lap. He thought he owned the place. Shame he couldn't help me get things organized. But as I sat there I realized I had already taken that first step. I was certainly ready to at least try to make some changes, some very overdue changes.

I fell asleep that night with Moxie by my side. I looked over at Horace the timekeeper. He was sound asleep. I let the tick tock of his clock lull me to sleep. Maybe this really was going to be my year—the year of Mary.

Planning Your Journey to Freedom from Disorganization

Grab your favorite beverage, sit quietly in your chair, and start filling-in your own chart below. Include all your monsters. Don't be afraid to cross out and make a correction—that is all part of the process. Mary had to make her own corrections and face her monsters, too. Below is a copy of her napkin for your use.

1. List the PROS of getting yourself or your home organized. What will you be able to do when you're organized that you can't do now? How will being organized make you feel?

2. List the CONS of getting organized. What's keeping you from doing what's required to get organized, right now? What benefits do you get from keeping things the way they are? Remember, be honest with yourself.

> *What will you be able to do when you're organized that you can't do now? How will being organized make you feel?*

Should I Get My Life Organized—Or Not?

Pros	Cons

So how did that exercise work for you? Do the pros of taking the next steps to getting organized outweigh the cons of staying the way you are? If you answered yes, then you have taken the first step on the road to organization.

Now that you've decided to embark on your own organizational path, you'll need to choose your destination(s) and set reasonable timeframes in which to get there. Use the below worksheet.

My Journey to an Organized Life—Timeline

My Destinations (the end results I want):	Start On:	Complete By:

Take a look at the list you just made. Evaluate each of your desired destinations to see if it is on **POINT**. Ask yourself, is it:

- ✓ **Purposeful**. Will it help you be able to live the kind of life you want to live?
- ✓ **Obtainable**. Do you have the time, skill, money, or other resources to achieve it?
- ✓ **Important to me**. Are you doing this because *you* want to do it, or only to please someone else?
- ✓ **Named**. Are the results you want specific enough that you'll know when you have achieved them?
- ✓ **Targeted in time**. When will you start, and when will you arrive at each destination?

Like Mary, you may discover that one or more of your desired destinations are simply not on ***POINT***—not realistic at this time. Postpone or eliminate those destinations from your list; you can always come back to them at a later time. Then, assign a start-on date and a complete-by date to each of your destinations.

The clock is still ticking, but now you're choosing to be in control of how you will spend your time going forward. So plan your work, and then start working your plan. You will be well on your way to cleaning the monsters out of your home without sprays!

TIME TO TANGO
January 3rd, 2000

I woke in the morning late as always. My clock radio was blaring the day's weather forecast—snow for the morning commute. The expected accumulation was reported to be six to eight inches. Since I had already hit the snooze button several times, this unexpected weather occurrence was going to turn my morning drive to work into one of hellish proportions. Spring couldn't get here soon enough.

I didn't even bother to hurry and get dressed. I was already doomed to be late for work—again. Moxie must have wandered off somewhere in the night, but Glums and Fiasco were lying in bed with me. They often came to visit me in bed in the mornings, especially on the days I had to work. I gave them each a well-deserved scratch behind the ears. Poor Glums meowed a lot as if trying to talk and make sense of what he saw but couldn't hear around him. Crazy Fiasco was contorted in an odd position. He was lying on his back with his paws straight up in the air. His head was half-covered in blankets. He was a mess from the day we brought him home from the shelter. He fit right in.

I could hear Horace down in the kitchen making coffee. Every morning at 7am, since I can remember,

I have woken-up to the smell of coffee in the house. Last year, Nadine gave Horace a coffee maker for Christmas. It came with an auto-on switch so you could set it to brew at a certain time each morning. Horace never needed to use the switch. He always brewed coffee at 7am.

When I arrived downstairs, Horace was peering out the window holding his steaming cup of coffee. The snow was already lying on the lawn in heaps, and it didn't look like it was going to stop any time soon.

"You might as well just hunker down," Horace said turning as he heard me walk into the kitchen. He of course was fully showered and dressed. "I don't think anyone is going anywhere this morning. I doubt the museum will open and need you there. From the sound of the news it seems everything is closing down. I'm going to work from home today."

I was checking my phone messages as he spoke. Sure enough, there was a message from Joe, my boss. "It looks like I will be working from home with you," I said to Horace. "No docents are needed at the museum today. It will be closed to visitors."

Horace gave me a quizzical look. He knew I didn't work from home. I couldn't smell the smoke from the gears grinding in his head, but he sure looked at me like he was trying to decipher what I was talking about.

I decided to drop the bomb. "I've made, and hopefully will stick to, a New Year's resolution this year."

"You are going to be a virtual docent working from home and giving tours? Is there some new museum technology you didn't mention?" He looked as confused as ever. The bomb was about to explode.

"No," I took a deep breath. "I made a list of some things I would like to accomplish around the house, and this kitchen is one of the things that needs to be addressed. We have no more room."

Horace still looked a little confused.

"I have a closet full of clothes which haven't seen the light of day in years. I don't even know if they fit. We have a garage that is meant to hold two cars and we can't even squeeze in one. I have papers everywhere in my corner of the home office that belong in the recycle bin, and I have an exercise bike that is currently being used as a clothes hanger."

Horace was staring at me. I was either going to cry or hyperventilate. The idea of everything I had written down on my chart yesterday was now as overwhelming as ever. It felt like an elephant was sitting on my chest. But I continued on. "Horace, I am ready to make a change. I just don't know how. I can't live like this anymore."

Horace put his cup down, pulled out a kitchen chair, and motioned for me to sit down. He pulled out the chair next to mine and tucked in. He clasped his hands together in front of him. He looked just like he does when he opens the credit card bill. The bomb had blown.

"Where is this list?" Horace said calmly.

I pulled a folded piece of paper from my robe pocket, laid it on the table, and smoothed out the creases with the palm of my hand. Horace looked it over, got up, poured a cup of coffee, handed it to me, and then sat back down. "This is a lot of work."

"Yes, so I wanted to get started right away. Since I'm off today, I thought I could make some good progress."

"And what makes today any different than yesterday or tomorrow?"

I was staring at him. He was teasing me. He didn't believe me. "I can do this all by myself!"

"I don't doubt that you can, but if you try to do it all at one time I will have to follow you around with a paper bag. Breathe already and drink your coffee. Let's see if there isn't something we can do here."

Horace got up and grabbed a pad of sticky notes and a blank piece of paper from the kitchen desk. He sat back down, took the pen from his pocket, and started to scribble words on the sticky notes. Then he drew a chart with the days of the week on one side of the paper and the time of day at the top.

"What are you doing?" I asked with casual interest while sipping my coffee. I swore I wouldn't need to breathe into a paper bag.

"We use a technique at work called time blocking. The secretary can move clients and meetings around on our software scheduling program depending on who is available at what time. You can do the same thing with sticky notes to block out time to work on your priorities for the week. If something comes up, just peel the sticky note off and move it to another place on your chart."

There was no explosion. Horace was actually helping me. He really did know how to manage time.

"Start by blocking out time for the things you've already committed to doing, like your job and any scheduled appointments. Then block out time to work on your other priorities, like organizing, taking care of the house, time with Nadine, time with me, and time to take care of yourself."

MY WEEKLY SCHEDULE	Morning 7:00 8:00 9:00 10:00 11:00	Afternoon 12:00 1:00 2:00 3:00 4:00	Evening 5:00 6:00 7:00 8:00 9:00
Monday	Work	Work	Laundry
Tuesday	Organizing	Organizing	Exercise
Wednesday	Work	Work	Shopping & Errands
Thursday	Organizing	Organizing	Exercise
Friday	Work	Work	Date Night!
Saturday	Household Chores	Organizing	Family Time
Sunday	Family Time	Family Time	Planning & Desk Time

I almost fell off the chair. "Why didn't you show me how to do this before?"

"You weren't ready. It seems now you are."

He had a point. He always had a point. "Now that you mention it, I have been ready for tango lessons, too." I smiled.

"Yes, and so maybe you should make a sticky note and we can work that in once or twice a month, assuming you have something to wear and we can make it on time."

I had plenty to wear! "You'll support me?"

"You have lots of support, and it seems I'm not the only one."

I looked down to see Moxie purring at my feet, but I don't think that is who Horace was referencing. Nadine was already pulling a chair up to the table and taking quite an interest in what we were discussing.

"I can help with your closet, Mom. I love clothes, oh, and shoes. Anything you don't want I get first dibs on, and when we get the closet purged of all the clothes you don't want we can go shopping for even MORE!"

Horace rubbed his forehead in contemplation. I knew the Christmas credit card bill hadn't come yet. The mailman probably wouldn't make it out today in the snow so I had at least one more day before that bomb exploded.

"It would be nice if you helped me while you are on holiday break, Nadine, but I think your father and I also need to have a conversation about the spending around here. I don't know if sticky notes are the answer to that problem, but I'm sure your father can come up with a plan." I smiled at Horace as I said that. I even patted his hand. Maybe it was my turn to offer *him* a paper bag?

Moxie jumped up on the kitchen table and sat on my sticky note chart. The clock chimed eight.

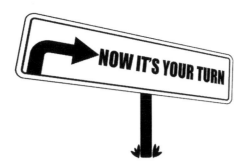

Freedom from the Unimportant: Organizing Your Time

Now it's time to decide WHEN you'll commit the time to take your organizing journey. Like Mary, you have many roles and responsibilities. You can't, and shouldn't plan to work on organizing 24/7! By using

You can't, and shouldn't plan to work on organizing 24/7!

time blocking, Mary built specific times into her weekly routine to work on her organizing priorities. She also designated specific times during the week to work on her other roles and responsibilities. On the chart below, check off the roles and responsibilities you currently have.

My Roles and Responsibilities

___ Work (outside the home)
___ Spouse/Partner
___ Parent
___ Home Manager (shopping, laundry, cleaning, etc.)
___ Home Administrator (bill paying, etc.)
___ Volunteer
___ Time for Me (exercise, hobbies, friends)
___ Student
___ Friend
___ Other _____
___ Other _____

Over the course of a week, it's important to allocate some time to tasks related to each of your roles and responsibilities. Using Mary's sticky note system, create one or more sticky notes for each of your roles and responsibilities. Use the blank copy of Mary's sticky note chart on page 25, or create your own.

First, block off time for any fixed appointments (your job, doctor's appointments, exercise classes, children's activities, etc.). Check your calendar to make sure you haven't forgotten about any scheduled appointments.

Next, block off time for any roles and responsibilities you noted above. If you need to work in shorter time blocks, you can further subdivide the morning, afternoon, and evening time blocks into hourly time periods.

Go back to the *My Journey to an Organized Life* worksheet. Make sure you block off time to work on your listed organizing projects!

MY WEEKLY SCHEDULE	Morning 7:00 8:00 9:00 10:00 11:00	Afternoon 12:00 1:00 2:00 3:00 4:00	Evening 5:00 6:00 7:00 8:00 9:00
Monday			
Tuesday			
Wednesday			
Thursday			
Friday			
Saturday			
Sunday			

CLEANING THE MONSTERS OUT OF THE HOUSE-WITHOUT SPRAYS

Still . . . January 3rd, 2000

I had just finished my shower and was getting dressed when I heard Horace taking a call in the home office. As I peeked out the window, the beauty of the earlier snow had now turned into a raging storm. The wind was whipping against the house and winter was letting us know it was here in full force.

Nadine was extremely excited to get into my closet. And while most people fear the monster under their bed, I was afraid of the one that was alive and well in my closet—hopefully he was still asleep.

I was wondering where Horace was with the paper bag. I needed to breathe. Nadine was like a shark attacking anything that was swimming around in my closet. Hopefully she would find the monster first. It wouldn't stand a chance against Nadine.

She had turned on the radio and was emptying everything out of my closet to the beat of her songs. She was making piles on the bed. I was overwhelmed. "Nadine, what are you doing? Stop it!"

I buried my head in my hands as I sat on the bed. I couldn't do it; it was just too much. I felt Nadine's arms around me just then; she was giving me a hug. In the background, Sarah McLachlan's song "Angel" played on the radio. I hugged Nadine back. She was always my angel. Tears were welling up in my eyes. Poor Glums and Fiasco jumped off the bed. They were drowning in clothes.

"Nadine, my closet is a mess! My room is a mess! Now my bed is a mess!" I was tired and frustrated. That monster must still be in the closet.

"Okay," she said. "But it doesn't *have* to be a mess, right?"

"I just can't do it."

"Mom, let's get rid of the mess. First, we need to move out the things that just don't belong in your clothes closet so we can make room for what belongs in there—your clothes."

Nadine removed a vacuum cleaner and several piles of books I had stacked in my closet. I think I saw her take out some wrapping paper, too. And I saw her moving out scrapbooking supplies. Where did all that come from?

"Mom, these things need to go somewhere else. Let's set them out in the hall and we'll take care of putting them away later," Nadine said as she looked over for my approval.

 I nodded. She was right.

Nadine grabbed a piece of blank paper from Horace's nightstand. In big letters down the side she wrote, *MESS*. Then she pinned it to my closet door with a thumbtack that had been holding my belts on the door.

"You want to get rid of the mess?" she said.

"Yes."

"Then let's examine what we have left in this archeological dig. We don't want you living in the eighties. We'll sort everything into piles of similar items—all shirts together, all pants together, and all sweaters together. That will make it easier for you to see what you have and make decisions on what to keep."

We continued working for what seemed like hours, but Nadine said it had only been 45 minutes. The piles of pants, jeans, shirts, and sweaters were turning into towers on, and around, my bed.

"Mom, these piles are getting pretty big. Maybe we should start to make some decisions about what you want to keep," Nadine said, at what seemed like just the right time.

"Alright," I replied.

"Okay Mom, let's start with this sweater pile. Ask yourself with each item you go through: does this fit, do I like wearing it, and is it in good shape? Okay? Nothing goes back in the closet unless it can pass those rules. If there is anything you don't want, sort it to a consign pile or donate bag so we can drop those items off next time we go out. How about we use these black lawn bags for donations and these white kitchen bags for those items we are taking to consignment? I'm going to start to take what you want to keep and fold or hang it up in the closet. I will put like things together so you can find them."

"If I get stuck will you help me decide what looks nice?"

"Yes. Like, look at this pink and white polka dot shirt. I've never even seen you wear this, and it's a good thing. Look at it!" Nadine held the shirt like it had the plague. Then she held up a gorgeous silk blouse for me to look at. "Sweet, I've never seen you wear this. The tags are still on it."

"It doesn't fit."

"Then we can put it in the consign bag. See, move it out."

As I started on the sweater pile, Nadine started writing on my MESS sign.

"Check this out, Mom. Here are your organizing rules in case you forget. I think I saw a list like this on one of those daytime talk shows you're always watching."

Move out items that don't belong.
Examine one category of items at a time.
Set rules for what you will and won't keep.
Systematize how you put things away: like things together, and stored close to where you'll use them.

We worked through the closet for hours, actually, another 45 minutes according to Nadine. There were piles of clothes everywhere, but Nadine was doing a great job of putting things back, and I had several full bags of clothes to donate to charity, plus several items I wanted to try to sell at the consignment shop. I was tired, hungry, and losing patience. We still had a lot of work to do. Nadine kept at it: dancing, singing, and putting things away in my closet. There was a song playing, "All Star," by some group called Smash Mouth? I was learning a lot about music today.

Nadine was putting things away systematically. I peeked my head in the closet and she had put all my shirts on the left side bar in the closet, by color, and all my pants on the right side bar, again, by color. A few of my skirts were hung near my pants, and it looked like she was pairing my suit jackets with their matching skirts. Now that she set up this system for me, I was pretty sure I could follow it when I put things away in the future.

"I'm tired, Nadine. I think it's time for a break."

"Okay, but you only get one hour for lunch."

We went down to the kitchen and I made some grilled cheese sandwiches. Nadine was busy listening to her music. Horace had come in the kitchen at the smell of food.

"You look exhausted," he smiled.

"You should see the bed," I smiled back, but with a look of horror on my face.

"Is Nadine hanging in there with you?"

"Yes, she gets first dibs on anything that doesn't fit or that I want to donate, and she gets 100% of the proceeds from anything I sell at consignment. I think she needs to go back to school. This is a hard deal. And she insists that we finish the closet after lunch and the kitchen tomorrow while she is here to help me. My closet is taking FOREVER! I can't imagine how long it will take to organize this kitchen."

"You have support. Take one step at a time. Let Nadine help you with your closet and when the closet is finished you can concern yourself with the kitchen. The kitchen has waited this long; it can wait a little longer. If you can organize that closet of yours, you can certainly handle this kitchen. Personally, I think you have accomplished a lot in just one morning!"

"Yes, and you have grilled cheese."

"And tango lessons," he pointed to the chart on the table. He had been messing around with my sticky notes and penciled in "tango" for Friday nights.

Hmmm, so that is the way he wanted to play the game. I grabbed a sticky note and posted it to the current evening's block on the chart. I showed off some of my new time management skills. It read, *Horace make dinner.*

P.S. KEEPING IT REAL AND HONEST
February 25th, 2000 (It has been some time since I last checked-in.)

As usual, my goal to tackle the kitchen right after my closet did not quite pan out by the date I had planned. Horace was right though; the kitchen finally got organized. It just took some time.

Work had become busy as the museum received a generous endowment from one of our patrons. I was exhausted. I just didn't have time for the kitchen. (It was hard enough keeping up with my newly organized clothes closet!) Now that everything in my closet was organized, I wanted it to stay that way, so I had to schedule time to keep up with laundry each week and put my clothes away where they belonged. The cats weren't sure where to sleep anymore as the clothing piles in my bedroom were no more. It felt good having my clothes and closet organized.

Nadine knew I was working a lot more, and we were also busy trying to sort through her college choices. We had taken a few college tours on the weekends, and of course, I forgot to block out the appropriate time on my sticky note time management chart. I was trying to stay organized with my appointments and time; I just got so busy.

Nadine was a big help and support in the kitchen. She gave me a few hours on her weekends, her time she would normally spend with friends, to help me organize the kitchen using the *MESS* formula. I was grateful and let her know, and she let me know she was grateful for the time I spent with her looking at colleges. In the process of organizing the kitchen, she boxed a lot of my duplicate items, as well as many of the kitchen items I *currently* use, to take with her to college. (There is always a price!) So my kitchen was well organized and purged, though later than I anticipated and planned, and everything that Nadine didn't box up to take to college had its own place. Now that I could see the entire floor and the cleared counter space, it was apparent the kitchen was in need of more than just organizing—it needed some updates.

The tile floor and countertops were pretty worn and ready for replacement. Nadine suggested I get new bake ware, dishes, and pots and pans since she confiscated my old ones. It looks like another shopping spree at the outlets, though I have seen some really nice cooking sets on some of the shopping channels. I love getting new things! I like the UPS man! I hate the credit card bills.

Freedom from Clutter: Organizing Your Rooms and Storage Areas

Are your closet and kitchen a mess like Mary's? Do your challenges with clutter involve other things like a large quantity of books, craft supplies, recipes, or magazines containing projects you say you would like to do . . . someday?

Regardless of the nature of your mess, you can use the same 4-step *MESS* formula Mary used to plan your attack. Begin with your highest-priority organizing project, the first one you listed in the *My Journey to an Organized Life* worksheet.

*M*ove out items that don't belong

You have already established a goal for the first area you want to organize. Any items that don't help you achieve that goal need to live somewhere else. *Somewhere else* might be

- in another room in your house;
- with their rightful owner;
- in a bag for charity; or
- in the trash or recycle bin.

As you come across items that don't belong in the area you are organizing, simply move them to another area to get them out of your way. At the end of your organizing session, relocate those items to their proper locations.

*E*xamine one category of items at a time

Mary was overwhelmed when Nadine started piling clothes on her bed randomly. A better approach is to evaluate one category of items at a time. If you're overrun by books, for example, you could start by gathering all gardening books together, choosing your favorites to keep, and eliminating the rest. When you examine one category of items at a time, the decision process becomes much more manageable.

> *When you examine one category of items at a time, the decision process becomes much more manageable.*

Set rules for what you will and won't keep

Having too many things is what causes most of our clutter problems in the first place. Having fewer things to keep organized will be a huge step in helping you achieve your organizing goals. This is your chance to rule over your clutter, rather than have your clutter rule over you. You're in charge! You can set the rules for what stays and what goes.

Here are some sample rules you might want to set for eliminating items. Discard:

- things that are torn, broken, worn out, or that you have no immediate plans to repair;
- clothes you haven't worn in ___ years;
- clothes that don't fit your current size or your current lifestyle;
- books and magazines you'll never read or read again;
- crafts you no longer enjoy or have time for and recipes you'll never make;
- kitchen gadgets you don't use;
- things you simply don't like—including gifts you've received;
- things you like but don't have room to keep; and
- things that keep you from living an organized life.

Systematize how you put things away—like things together, stored close to where you'll use them

There are two objectives for putting anything away: The first is to be able to easily retrieve it when you need it; the second is to have a home for it when you aren't using it. Follow these two simple storage rules and you'll be able to do just that:

1. Store Like Things Together

Here are a few examples of *like things* you might store together:

- clothing (shirts, pants, sweaters, belts, shoes);

- kitchen items (cooking, baking, eating, storage containers, food);

- garage/basement items (automotive, sporting goods, tools);

- files (vital documents, tax-related, medical records, financial, personal interests, memorabilia); and

> *There are two objectives for putting anything away: The first is to be able to easily retrieve it when you need it; the second is to have a home for it when you aren't using it.*

- papers requiring action (unpaid bills, medical insurance claims to file, phone calls to make).

Feel free to create your own definitions of *like* things. For example, it might be more meaningful for you to store your clothing by purpose (business, casual, formal) or by color (all the blue clothes together, regardless of their type).

2. Store Things Close to Where You'll Use Them

No offense, but we're all basically lazy. If it's too hard to put things away we simply don't do it, and clutter is the result. Here are some examples of where to store items.

- Clothing: Store the current season's clothes in the most accessible places in your closet.

- Kitchen: Store cooking items near the stove, baking items near the oven, plates and silverware near the table, storage containers near a countertop, and food in the pantry.

- Garage and basement items: Store automotive supplies near the car, sporting goods near the door, and tools near the tool bench.

Creating storage space for things close to where you use them is your best hope for maintaining organization in your home. Not only will you be able to find things when you need them, you'll be more likely to return them to their appropriate space when finished with them.

SWINGING OVER THE MONEY PIT-A ROPE PLEASE
February 25th, 2000

Let's face it, I know myself better than anyone. I know what the credit card bills look like—all three! In fact, I named them after my cats:

1. VISA's Got Moxie

This card had the lowest balance. I did my best to pay it off with lots of vigor and effort! Now I make sure I pay off the balance each month.

2. American Express Glums

It had a high balance, but it made me feel happy to buy things so I used it to cheer myself up. I would act like Glums when I got the bill; I didn't listen to the collection phone calls (couldn't hear them) or read the collection notices when a payment was overdue.

3. Discover The Fiasco

It was out of control with no boundaries as to the purchases I made on it, in other words, every shopping network and catalog company knew about Fiasco.

And yes, each month when the credit card bills came, just like all the other mail I received on a daily basis, I would take them upstairs (when I got around to it) and dump them on my home office desk. The papers had spread out like a virus and had fallen to various places all over the floor. And I can tell you monsters were still in my house, waiting and watching; they still laughed at me from time to time. The papers and bills were the loudest, in fact, I think the monsters that were living in the kitchen and my closet moved to my home office—it was pretty chaotic in there. My nice, leather, swivel computer chair had receipts sticking out of every possible fold. I had no idea where it all came from.

Then I would look over at Horace's desk in the corner. It wasn't perfect, but it wasn't cluttered. Yes, his desk had lots of electronic gizmos on it (he liked to buy and tinker with electronics), but I didn't know how he maintained an organized desk. I could do it at work, well, I had to do it at work; I just didn't feel like doing it at home. I would get overwhelmed with the mail, the paper, and the bills and I had no idea how to maintain my scrapbooking supplies. There wasn't any time to organize and I hated doing it! And even though Horace and I had made time to take our tango lessons once a month, and it was *really* great, I knew why I avoided the home office for so long. Like I said, I knew myself better than anyone. It was overwhelming.

That is when Horace and I would really fight. Not just the tick-tock-why-aren't-you-ready-and-on-time fights, I'm talking down-and-dirty-head-butting fights. It was why I had avoided the conversations about bills, budgets, and savings. It was why he had, too. But I had made a resolution to change this year, well, at least to try to change. And I knew Nadine couldn't help us with everything. In fact, I didn't want her to know. I felt like a child. Horace and I hadn't saved anything but the retirement monies that were automatically deducted from his paycheck and deposited into his 401(k) account each month. I didn't make very much working part-time at the museum. I was hoping Nadine would find scholarships for college. Every year I had wanted to save—it just never happened. The new kitchen counter tops and floor—they would never happen. We already had a home equity line we paid on each month because we had to replace the roof and gutters about two years ago.

Since Horace and I didn't talk about money, it surely made things worse. In fact, anytime we did have a conversation about money I got a terrible headache. He had tried to approach me about the Christmas spending, and he had tried to tell me for years we needed to save for Nadine and her college expenses. We've had to pay lots of interest and overdraft fees (not to mention the years we had to file for tax deadline extensions)—he tried, and he tried, and he got nowhere. I knew he was stressed. He had given up. We both had. It was probably why he had been spending so much time, and money, at the club house. But, Nadine and her education were important enough to make me ready, and Horace and I had to come to a happy medium. That is why we finally got professional help. There were things I needed to finally address on my own with a therapist, there were things we had to work on as a couple in counseling, and there were things a financial planner (Horace's friend) recommended to help get us on the right financial track. The only thing I have to say . . . I wish we would have done it sooner. It helped prepare both of us for what we needed to see in ourselves so we could tackle our relationship and finances—it helped a lot.

Actually, Horace had the knowledge all along—after all, he is the financial guru. Like I said, *we* needed some help. We could finally sit together, just once a month for a specific period of time, and work on our money management and bills. Horace had suggested we make a list of our goals, by priority, with an achieve-by-date. With Horace's help, our goals were right on *POINT*. Horace liked to use his computer, so, it looked like this when it was printed.

My Personal Financial Goals	Priority	Cost	Achieve By
Pay Off Credit Card Balances	1	$22,500	June 2002
Nadine's College Expenses	2	$48,000	Don't know how we're going to do this
Kitchen Renovations	3	$8,000	After college is paid for
25th Anniversary Vacation (To South America to tango!)	4	$6,000	We may have to rethink this

Horace and I then took a look at *The Good*, that is, what income was coming in each month. Horace made some spreadsheets, remember, financial guru.

The Good

Income Sources (after taxes & other deductions)	Monthly Amount
Horace's Work	$9,375
Mary's Work	$1,250
Total Spendable Monthly Income	**$10,625**

Then, together, we looked at *The Bad*—our three credit cards.

The Bad

Creditors (for Unsecured Debts)	Total Outstanding Balance	Minimum Monthly Payment	Interest Rate%
VISA's Got Moxie	0		
American Express Glums	$7,500	$75	22%
Discover The Fiasco	$15,000	$150	16%
Total Minimum Monthly Payments (Use this amount to complete the next chart.)	**$22,500**	**$225**	

Then we looked at the ugly monsters. There was the home equity loan and the new car we had to get when Nadine got her license and confiscated my old Honda. (It was really okay—I had a new car with a sun roof and leather seats!) Horace happened to have a spreadsheet on file at work for budgeting. (He was trying to shove it in my face for many years. Tick tock. I really liked being my own budget clock! It was much more fun.) Anyway, I'm glad Horace was there to hold my hand. We were still working on certain things, but I was ready to confront the ugly monsters and make some changes.

The Ugly

Expenses	Monthly Amount $
Auto & Transportation:	
Auto Loan Payment(s)	415
Gasoline	100
Auto Service & Maintenance	50
Auto Registration	12
Auto Insurance	100
Tolls	
Parking	
Public Transportation	
Bank Fees:	
ATM Fees	20
NSF & Late Fees	25
Bills & Utilities:	
Total Minimum Monthly Payment on Unsecured Debts	225
Alimony Payable	
Mortgage Payment (principal and interest only)	1250
Home Equity Loan Payment	350
Rent	
Storage Unit Rent	
Home, Yard, & Pool Maintenance	1000
Homeowner's or Renter's Insurance	100
Homeowner's Association Fee	
Home Phone	50
Internet	
Mobile Phone(s)	100
Television	75
Electricity	125
Gas	75
Security System	
Sewer	
Water	10
Cash Withdrawals	600
Charity Donations	
Education:	
Books & Supplies	
Tuition	
Entertainment:	
Activities	500
Music & Movies	
Newspaper & Magazine Subscriptions	125
Financial:	
Organizing	
Accountant	20
Life Insurance Premiums	25
Long Term Care Insurance Premiums	

Expenses	Monthly Amount $
Food:	
Groceries	600
Dining Out (includes fast food, coffee, & alcohol)	300
Gifts Given	225
Health & Fitness (if not withheld from paycheck):	
Health Insurance	
Dental Insurance	
Rx Insurance	
Vision Insurance	
Medical Bills (amount not covered by insurance)	25
Dental Bills (amount not covered by insurance)	
Pharmacy Bills (amount not covered by insurance)	15
Eye Care Bills (amount not covered by insurance)	30
Gym & Sports Club Memberships	1850
Sports	
Kids' Expenses:	
Allowance	100
Childcare	
Child Support	
Kids' Activities	200
Toys	
Personal Care:	
Hair & Nails	250
Laundry & Dry Cleaning	50
Spa & Massage	
Pet Care	350
Shopping:	
Books	100
Clothing	750
Electronics & Software	150
Hobbies	100
Household Items	500
Sporting Goods	100
Taxes:	
Estimated Federal Tax Payments	
Estimated State Tax Payments	
Property Tax	
Travel:	
Hotel	
Transportation	
Vacation Activities	100
Contributions to Savings (if not withheld from paycheck):	
Retirement	
College	
Targeted Savings (for vacation, home improvements, etc.)	
Rainy Day Savings	
Total Monthly Expenses:	**$11,547**

Then we looked at what we had left over each month. It was then that I really needed to breathe into a paper bag. WOW! What a reality check!

The Reality Check

Total Spendable Monthly Income	$10,625
Total Monthly Expenses	$11,547
Total Monthly Excess Income (or Deficiency)	($ 922)

Not only had we been overspending by almost $1,000 each month, we had to come up with a way to cut back if we wanted to make true headway, save, and reach any of our financial goals. It was getting uglier by the minute.

Horace looked over the spreadsheets. "We need to cut spending. The shopping and clothing bills are through the roof, not to mention the trips you and Nadine make to the salon for your hair and nails. And what are you buying for the cats each month?"

I looked at him in shock. I think I started to tremble. What happened to working as a team? "What about your golf membership fees? And let's not forget your electronics habit!"

"Well, at least I use and enjoy my membership. You buy books and magazines that you never read and I haven't seen you use any of the scrapbooking supplies you continue to buy and bring into the house. Don't forget what you have stored in the garage." He remained so calm.

"I can't see what is in the garage. I feel like I am in a golf store every time I go in there!"

"You are exaggerating," Horace said emotionless.

I was FULL of emotion. "Then explain to me why, when we never go out much at all together and we can barely find the time for dance lessons, so much is being spent on entertainment and eating out?" I could feel my face turning red.

"Mary, we both buy lunch and breakfast on work days," replied the lips of Mr. Tick Tock Matter-of-Fact.

"Yes, but I put my charges on the credit card and I don't blow the big bucks at the club house, so why do we have $600 a month in ATM withdrawals?"

"Are you denying you ever take money out of the ATM?"

He was still so serious, but he was right. "No, I do, but not $600!"

"Neither do I but together it seems we are."

Horace was looking pale. *Take the emotion out of it. Fighting gets you nowhere. Act like an adult.* "I'm sorry Horace, I just had no idea how bad it was."

"That is why we have to do this, Mary. We have to make a change. And you are right, it isn't just you. I am responsible for part of this, too. Maybe I should quit the golf club for a bit."

"Horace, you don't have to give it up entirely. Maybe you can just switch to a less expensive club? I know you like the one you are a member of, but it would save us a lot right there."

"And the shopping and salon visits? I can meet you halfway." His reply, as his eyebrows shot up over his eyeglass rims, was not what I expected.

"Yes, let's make a budget that cuts our discretionary spending in half. Nadine and I can cut out some of our beauty visits. And you are right; we don't need any more cat supplies. They just look so cute. I can cut back on buying clothes. It may be time for me to find something else to do other than shop. Are you still open to setting parental controls on the TV?"

Horace managed a smile. "I can look into that. In fact, we can look into cutting back on our TV channel subscription, and I can set up automation so our bills are paid on time and we will never have to pay late fees. I should balance the checkbook each month, too. Do you think you can cancel some of the magazines you don't read? Even if we just cut them in half it would be better."

"Yes, if you can cut back on new golfing supplies and electronic gadgets. And we both need to do something about the ATM and eating out."

"And the credit card," Horace said as he took my hand. "We have to stop the bleeding, Mary. Let's work out a budget and give ourselves a cash allowance each month—but we have to give the credit cards a break. You see the interest we are paying? By only paying the minimum balance on our credit cards each month we will never pay them off. We are slaves to our debt."

Sadly, he was correct. "Yes, we would have money to pay for the trip we want to take and the kitchen renovations."

Horace's face lit up. "Think bigger, Mary. With all of these changes we could pay off our credit cards, save, send our daughter to college, and still treat ourselves to the things we want. We just can't do it all at one time."

"I can't give it all up."

"We don't have to. We'll both have to make some concessions, but just like your closet and kitchen organization it won't happen overnight, it will take time. But we can work and support each other. We'll sit down just once each month to talk finances and the rest of the month we will work hard to just cut-back and stay on track. We can't talk about it all the time and worry over it or we'll get nowhere. We can still eat out and take dance lessons and we can still golf and shop; we just have to do it in moderation. Agreed?" He put out his hand waiting for me to shake it.

"Agreed," I said. Tears were streaming down my face; this was going to be the hardest change I ever had to make in my life. But as I said, I wanted more than a house; I wanted a home. And that home included more than just stuff, it included Horace, and happiness, and a daughter who could have friends over. Clean and white. Horace and I were making *our* home.

Freedom from Financial Chaos: Organizing How You Spend Your Money

If you are financially disorganized you may already have experienced some of these financial consequences: late fees, overdraft fees, finance charges, poor credit ratings, overdue notices from the IRS, or even foreclosure on your home. Financial disorganization brings negative personal consequences, too: marital discord, the inability to plan and save for the future, and the health risks of associated stress. Becoming financially organized will have the same kinds of positive effects on your life that you experience when your home is organized. As you begin to gain control of your money, you'll be able to spend or invest it to help you reach your personal goals. Begin by using Mary's 4-step financial organization road map.

Step 1: Identify Where You Want to Go

The first step toward financial organization is to identify your personal financial goals. If you are married, do this as a couple. List your goals in the chart below. Then rank them in order of priority, estimate their costs, and assign the dates by which you plan to achieve them.

My Personal Financial Goals	Priority	Cost	Achieve By

Test each of your goals to see if it is on *POINT*.

- ✓ **P**urposeful. Will achieving this financial goal help you be able to live the kind of life you want to live?
- ✓ **O**btainable. Given your circumstances, can you realistically achieve it?
- ✓ **I**mportant to me. Are you doing this because *you* want to do it, or only to please someone else?
- ✓ **N**amed. Are the results you want specific enough that you'll know when you have achieved them?
- ✓ **T**argeted in time. By when do you plan to achieve each goal?

Adjust your goals, prioritization, and achieve-by dates as needed.

Step 2: Identify Where You Are Today

Have you ever stepped on the bathroom scale after a week of indulging in too much rich food and drink? The number on the scale might have been painfully shocking; nevertheless, it was a number you needed to see if you intended to revert to a more healthy weight. Identifying your current income, debts, and expenses can feel like stepping on the bathroom scale. But in order to achieve the financial goals you have set, you first need to have a clear (although possibly unpleasant) picture of your current financial situation. Use the following tables to create a picture of your current financial situation.

The Good:

The Good includes your net spendable monthly income, including take-home pay (after deductions), pension, Social Security, and any additional income you receive (interest, dividends, alimony, child support, rents, etc.).

The Good

Income Sources	Monthly Amount
	$
	$
	$
	$
Total Spendable Monthly Income	$

The Bad:

The Bad is your unsecured consumer debt, including outstanding credit card balances, personal lines of credit, student loans, and any back taxes due.

The Bad

Creditors (for Unsecured Debts)	Total Outstanding Balance	Minimum Monthly Payment	Interest Rate %
Total Minimum Monthly Payments (Use this amount to complete the below chart)	$	$	

The Ugly:

The Ugly is the truth about how you have been spending your money. Take an average of your spending in each expense category for at least the past three months. Remember to include the amount you need to put aside every month to cover quarterly, semi-annual, and seasonal expenses you might not have incurred during the past three months.

The Ugly

Expenses	Monthly Amount
Auto & Transportation:	
Auto Loan Payment(s)	
Gasoline	
Auto Service & Maintenance	
Auto Registration	
Auto Insurance	
Tolls	
Parking	
Public Transportation	
Bank Fees:	
ATM Fees	
NSF & Late Fees	

Expenses	Monthly Amount $
Bills & Utilities:	
Total Minimum Monthly Payment on Unsecured Debts	
Alimony Payable	
Mortgage Payment (principal and interest only)	
Home Equity Loan Payment	
Rent	
Storage Unit Rent	
Home, Yard, & Pool Maintenance	
Homeowner's or Renter's Insurance	
Homeowner's Association Fee	
Home Phone	
Internet	
Mobile Phone(s)	
Television	
Electricity	
Gas	
Security System	
Sewer	
Water	
Cash Withdrawals	
Charity Donations	
Education:	
Books & Supplies	
Tuition	
Entertainment:	
Activities	
Music & Movies	
Newspaper & Magazine Subscriptions	
Financial:	
Organizing	
Accountant	
Life Insurance Premiums	
Long Term Care Insurance Premiums	
Food:	
Groceries	
Dining Out (includes fast food, coffee, & alcohol)	
Gifts Given	
Health & Fitness (if not withheld from paycheck):	
Health Insurance	
Dental Insurance	
Rx Insurance	
Vision Insurance	
Medical Bills (amount not covered by insurance)	
Dental Bills (amount not covered by insurance)	
Pharmacy Bills (amount not covered by insurance)	
Eye Care Bills (amount not covered by insurance)	
Gym & Sports Club Memberships	
Sports	

Expenses	Monthly Amount $
Kids' Expenses:	
Allowance	
Childcare	
Child Support	
Kids' Activities	
Toys	
Personal Care:	
Hair & Nails	
Laundry & Dry Cleaning	
Spa & Massage	
Pet Care	
Shopping:	
Books	
Clothing	
Electronics & Software	
Hobbies	
Household Items	
Sporting Goods	
Taxes:	
Estimated Federal Tax Payments	
Estimated State Tax Payments	
Property Tax	
Travel:	
Hotel	
Transportation	
Vacation Activities	
Contributions to Savings (if not withheld from paycheck):	
Retirement	
College	
Targeted Savings (for vacation, home improvements, etc.)	
Rainy Day Savings	
Total Monthly Expenses:	

The Reality Check:

It's time to do the math. Plug your total spendable monthly income and total monthly expenses into the chart below, and then subtract your expenses from your income.

The Reality Check

Total Spendable Monthly Income	
Total Monthly Expenses	
Total Monthly Excess Income (or Deficiency)	

Step 3: Identify the Changes in Spending You Will Make to Achieve Your Personal Financial Goals

First, congratulate yourself for getting this far along the path toward financial organization. You have already done half of the hard work! Now that you have an accurate picture of your financial situation and a prioritized list of your financial goals, you are ready to embark on the journey toward achieving those goals.

If Your Expenses Exceed Your Income

If you discovered that your current level of spending exceeds your income, your first priority will be to find ways to live within your means. Examine each of your expense categories to see where you can realistically cut back. For example, perhaps you can switch to basic cable and forego the premium channels. Are you paying rent to a storage company to store things you really don't need? Consider donating those items to charity (and taking the tax deduction) thus eliminating the need to pay for excess storage. If you find that you spend as much money dining out as you do on groceries, consider building time in your week to fix meals and snacks so you can reduce your food expenses. If you're not actually reading those magazines you subscribe to—cancel your subscriptions! Are you paying late fees because you forget to pay your bills? Sign up for automatic bill-pay to eliminate those fees (and simultaneously improve your credit rating). These are just a few examples of small steps you can take to reduce your expenses. Think of the places where you can easily reduce your spending without feeling terribly deprived.

If You Have Unsecured Debt

Unless you are earning more than 20%-24% in interest on your savings, it doesn't make a lot of financial sense to pay that percentage rate in finance charges on your unsecured debts. Paying off your credit card balances and personal loans is an easy way to start putting money in your pocket to use for your financial priorities. You will need to allocate some (or all) of your monthly excess income toward paying down your debt.

Here is one way to get those debts paid off; your financial advisor may have additional suggestions. For this example, let's assume you have an excess monthly income of $500 over your expenses.

From your Creditors chart (*The Bad*) above, locate the amount of your *total minimum monthly payment*.

For this example, we'll assume that your total minimum monthly payment on debt is $120. Since this amount has already been factored into your total monthly expenses, the new total monthly amount you'll be applying towards debt will be $620:

        $500   (monthly excess income to be applied to debt)

      + $120   (total minimum monthly payments on debt that you are already paying)

        $620   (new monthly amount to apply to your debt)

From your Creditors chart above, find the debt with the *lowest total outstanding balance*, regardless of the interest rate. In the example below, the creditor with the lowest total outstanding balance is the gasoline card.

Creditors (for Unsecured Debts)	Total Outstanding Balance	Minimum Monthly Payment
Bank Credit Card	$1,500	$15
Gasoline Card	$550	$10
Student Loan	$4,000	$75
Department Store Card	$1,000	$20
Total Minimum Monthly Payments	$7,000	$120

Pay the minimum balance on all debts *except* the one with the lowest total outstanding balance. In this example, during the first month you would pay only the minimum payments on the bank credit card ($15), student loan ($75), and department store card ($20), for a total of $110.

Apply the remaining $510 ($620-$110) to the gasoline card, significantly reducing its total outstanding balance to only $40. Paying off the debt with the lowest outstanding balance first will give you encouragement that you are making progress with taking control of your finances.

When one debt is satisfied, apply the excess over the total minimum payments due to the creditor with the *next-lowest total outstanding balance*. Repeat this process every month, as was shown in the gasoline card example, until all debts are paid in full.

As you are paying down your debt, it is important that you do not incur any new debt. Pay cash or use a debit card for purchases going forward.

Step 4: Take Steps to Achieve Your Financial Goals

You have worked very hard to get your finances in order so you can begin to save or spend your money on the people and things that are most important to you. Like most people, you will need to save money each month to reach your goals. Visit a financial planner for advice specific to your situation. While your money is busy working for you, there are additional steps you can take to make sure you stay on track.

Use two checking accounts—one for paying regular bills and the other for discretionary purchases. Do not carry checks or a debit card for the bill-paying account. This will prevent you from using that account for discretionary purchases.

- Set up automatic transfers or deposits into both checking accounts to make sure you will have enough money to cover planned expenses.

- Automate wherever possible. In addition to setting up automatic bill payments, you can schedule automatic transfers into savings or investment accounts to happen every pay day. Pay yourself first. You'll never miss the money if it isn't in your checking account in the first place.

- Reconcile your bank statements every month.

- Get up close and personal with where your money is going. Schedule time once a month to review your spending.

- If you share expenses with someone, save your money discussions for your monthly financial review time instead of arguing about each other's spending habits daily.

> *Get up close and personal with where your money is going. Schedule time once a month to review your spending.*

- Compare your actual spending to your planned spending. Does this sound like a budget? It is—and you already began to create it back in Step 2 when you filled in the expenses worksheet (*The Ugly*). Remember to adjust the amounts on the worksheet based on the lifestyle changes you have made and the debts you have paid off. Every month, compare your actual spending to your expenses worksheet (*The Ugly*).

- Revisit your financial goals at least once a year. How far have you come toward achieving them?

- Do you need to re-prioritize the list? Have any of your goals changed? Update your financial goals in writing.

- Visit your financial planner annually to make any needed changes.

Financial organization, like any type of organization, is a lifestyle, not an event. Just as keeping the rooms in your home organized reduces your stress level and frees you to use your home as you choose, keeping your finances organized frees you to work toward achieving your financial goals.

THE SECOND HONEYMOON
April 30th, 2000

Spring had sprung. It always does. Just when you aren't looking the leaves seem to take bud from nowhere, the flowers and colorful song birds come back with the warmer, fragrant air, and the pesky house flies make their way back into your kitchen. I had been trying to shoo a fly out all morning while I was sitting at the kitchen table planning a graduation party menu for Nadine. Moxie copied my arm movements hoping to catch, and surely eat, his prize. Up to that point, we were both unsuccessful.

Horace and I had spoken with Nadine. We decided to keep her celebration small and at home with a family-style cookout. Some family and several of Nadine's school friends were coming over. In just a few weeks she would finish school. I still couldn't believe it. And I couldn't believe Nadine wanted so many friends over. The kitchen wasn't looking like a showroom, but it was neat and clean and I had no qualms or fears about having company. I couldn't wait for an excuse to take my sister up and show her my bedroom. She had been on me for years to do something about my closet and clothes—she was in for a shock!

Nadine had decided to stick around and go to a local state college. Horace and I were thrilled with her choice as we didn't want to see her go, at least not yet, and the savings we needed to allot for college would be substantially less than we had previously planned. Nadine wanted to be a school teacher; Horace and I both knew how well suited to instruction she was—and very organized. She is creative too, but she didn't inherit my art gene. She has Horace's clockwork system wired in her brain. It serves her well.

The past two months were a little rocky at first, but Horace and I got into a groove with sitting down each month and going over financial matters. All of the changes we implemented, including putting away the credit cards for now, had worked in small, but amazing ways. It wasn't as much of a sacrifice as I had anticipated. I still had a budget to shop with, it just wasn't as much. With the warmer weather I had been spending more time outside when not at the museum. I had made some small progress in the garage, though it overwhelmed me and surely would look to most like I did nothing. Nadine needed to use her summer break to help us with that one!

Nadine stepped in again to help with organizing the papers in the home office. Well, the papers were originally on the kitchen desk, the dining room table, my nightstand, and I believe some found their way to the basement—and of course on the floor. I'm not sure how. (It must have been the monsters.) Now all the papers have a happy home in the office, though the office was bursting at the seams.

Horace sat with me and we discarded old papers he was sure we didn't need, like miscellaneous receipts from years ago and very old billing statements. We have never run a business from the home so none of our home expenses needed to be kept in our tax file for the accountant. (Horace explained that to me.) In the process of purging the old papers, Horace suggested having his part-time secretary, Alexis, come and help with some of the paper sorting. I was horrified! I couldn't imagine having someone from his office come to our house and see our mess. But Horace sat me down, before he needed to pull out the paper bag so I could catch my breath, and reminded me what Alexis was good at—what she could teach me. After all, she *is* the one who keeps Horace straight at work and has helped him to set up his work files. He assured me she was a patient teacher, just like Nadine, and that she enjoys helping people. I still wasn't sold on the idea, but I was willing to give it a shot.

Alexis was a godsend and worth the expenditure. In just a few working sessions, Alexis and I had purged and sorted through a good amount of papers in the office. She told me to think about things in a logical process and ask myself the **5-Ws**. **Why** do I need this paper? If I don't need to do anything with it right now, or save it for future reference, I can surely toss it. **Who** cares if I keep it? If no one else, like the tax man, needs me to keep it, and I don't have a good reason to keep it, I can toss it. I can't believe how many papers I had kept over the years because I thought I *had* to keep them. My "to shred" pile was huge! I thought anything that came in the mail with my name and address on it should be shredded. Identity theft is so common. But Alexis reminded me that anyone can find my name and address on the internet, and unless a document contained account numbers, pin numbers, financial information, or sensitive personal information it could go right into the recycle bin.

Then Alexis taught me to ask myself a question about each piece of paper that comes into my life: **What's** the next thing I need to do with this paper? Do I need to act on it in some way soon, or do I simply need to file it so I can find it in the future? I can't tell you how helpful that was! I had avoided dealing with my paperwork for so long—it was such a huge pile. But when I asked myself those questions about each piece of paper, I found that only a very small number of papers required my attention. Then we addressed the **when** and **where** of paper storage. If it was something I didn't need ready access to, it went to an archival storage file cabinet in the basement. Documents I frequently needed like my phone and e-mail list for work and blank insurance claim forms stayed in the desk in the home office.

Alexis also set up what she called an *action box*. In clear, see-through folders were all the papers I needed to take action on before I could discard or file them. Each folder had a label of action. I could grab a folder to make calls, pay bills, talk with Horace, talk with Nadine, and store papers for upcoming projects, like Nadine's graduation party and ideas for the kitchen counter tops!

Alexis suggested we color code my filing system. She said it helped her at Horace's office to quickly find things. We used green folders, the color of money, to hold financial documents; red folders (stop, caution, don't toss) to hold permanent and vital records; purple folders (alliteration of the letter *P* is easy to remember—plus my favorite color is purple) to hold documents for people and pets.

Alexis had Horace purchase some brown accordion folders, one for each tax year including the current year. Now all our tax returns and supporting documents had a home in case of audit. It will sure be a breeze when I can hand the accountant the expandable folder for 2000. It will make my life, and his, easier.

We also took a few 3-ring binders, one for Horace, one for Nadine, and one for me, and placed our medical records in them. Each family member now had their own individual medical record archive. I liked having a handy reference with all of Nadine's immunization records, especially since the college would be requesting them.

Instead of filing paper alphabetically, Alexis and I sorted by category. It made more sense to me to file that way, though Horace wasn't on board. Since I am the one who will be doing most of the filing, and Horace understands the color coding, I won out on that one!

Before Alexis and I finished, she reminded me that the 5-W process not only applies to physical paper, but to electronic files and documents as well. (Apparently she has had the same talk with Horace before, and on numerous occasions.) Electronic files can be named and you can drag and drop emails, or scan documents, into them. I think Horace is Alexis's work in progress.

We opened up a lot of new space around the house, and in the home office, by taking out the paper piles. I now keep fresh flowers on the dining room table in place of mail. It is my one little reward for keeping the table clear of papers. And we made enough room in the home office by clearing out and filing papers, my old magazines (now I only subscribe to five, though I am still thinking about cancelling a few), and some of Horace's electronic equipment to set up a little craft table. Some storage bins now house my scrapbooking supplies. As they are filled to the brim I'm currently not buying anymore supplies. I didn't realize how much I had until I saw it all organized together in one spot.

Horace put up a shelf in the home office where he keeps some of the books he doesn't want to part with. Now they are off the floor. His electronic gadgets were mostly out of date and he wasn't using them, so we donated what we could and he is using part of his bugeted monthly allowance to buy a gadget here and there when he feels so inclined. Though I still have some clutter on my desk, his desk looks amazing. It gives me an example to follow. I told Horace I like to work in a creative desk space, he said, "Creative does not equate to messy." Sadly, he was right. Isn't he always right?

Things in the office couldn't have worked out better for Glums, Moxie, and Fiasco. There is so much light that pours in through the windows—another reason I wanted to scrapbook in there. The cats now go there to lie in the sun. I leave the windows open and they jump up to sit in the sills and watch the birds fly by. It makes me happy to see Glums enjoying himself, especially since the UPS man doesn't visit as often as he used to with cat treats.

The UPS man did stop by the other day, though. I had to hide the package in my closet, which was hard to do at first because I had to take some clothes off the hangers to hide the box on the floor, but Horace wasn't the wiser. Our anniversary was a week away, and though I knew we had said we would stick to the budget, we were doing so well I wanted to buy him a special gift—an electronic range finder. It fit the bill as it was both golf and electronic related. These were Horace's two favorite hobbies. The technology is new as it works via satellite so it wasn't cheap, but we have been paying down the credit card bills just fine. It was just one expenditure of $650 that was about equal to my old monthly clothing expense habit. The South America trip was off for a few years so I wanted to make this anniversary special. I knew Horace would love the range finder.

A week later, when we were getting dressed to attend an end of the year awards banquet at school for Nadine, Horace asked me about the mound he saw on the floor of my closet. Our anniversary was two days off, but I just couldn't wait for the surprise.

"I know we agreed to keep things simple this year and follow our new budget plan, but our anniversary is just a few days away and we have been doing so well saving. I just wanted to get you something nice. You deserve it." I held out the box which I had wrapped in white paper with a silver lace bow.

"Mary, I am getting the impression this isn't a simple gift." Horace was always too serious. Surely, this was part of the reason his jet black hair was now going gray around his ears.

"We agreed not to give it all up, remember?"

"We aren't. We are spending in moderation." He gazed at the box as if it might be rigged with explosives. He was sort of correct on that one.

"Please open it."

"It is the thought Mary, not the material worth inside. We talked about this, remember? Not just with each other but with the therapist. We agreed. I am trying hard, too."

I didn't know how to respond. I took the box and opened it for him. He knew what it was as soon as he saw it.

"Mary, I love it, but just like everything else we have donated or given away around here I don't really need it." He held his hand out to me and directed me to sit on the bed. "Please send it back. We don't have the money to spend on gifts like this right now." Always calm, always so sure. "Don't take it personally."

"But I do."

"Well, then you will ruin my surprise, but it seems you have left me no choice." Horace walked over to his briefcase near his closet door. He pulled out what looked like paper, no, two tickets. What had he done!

"Horace, we can't afford to travel anywhere right now. We both agreed on that. What did you go and do?" I felt like shaking my finger at him, but I thought better and sat perfectly still. I wasn't doing so well with keeping my end of the spending on track either. I was not one to judge.

"We agreed to keep it simple. I took off work for our anniversary this week and I purchased two tickets to the zoo. Do you remember when we first met?"

I was beside myself. "Yes, we were in college and I had a summer job at the zoo working with kids in the art camp. You had an internship in the business office."

"Correct. And I believe it was somewhere near the tiger cage that I first met your eyes." He was doing his best to make me feel guilty as hell. He was succeeding.

"Yes, I remember. I was having lunch on the bench watching the tigers and you left your air conditioned office to take a stroll? That is the way you always told the story." He was smiling. He just kept rubbing it in.

"Go on."

"Some guys in accounting said they had seen a pretty brunette who was working in the summer camp with kids and that she often sat to eat lunch near the tigers." I played along.

"And then?"

"Won't we be late for Nadine's banquet?"

"No, we have plenty of time. Finish the story."

He would know; he is the clock. I was already dressed as it was much easier to find my clothes in the closet since Nadine and I organized it. I wasn't running late. "You had been hanging around the tigers for the whole week waiting to see the pretty brunette, but she never came."

"And why not?"

"Because you preferred blondes!"

"No, I prefer brunettes. You had recently dyed your hair blonde."

"And you had the audacity to ask me, while I sat on the bench minding my own business and eating lunch, where the brunette girl was that worked in the camp. I must know her as I was wearing a camp shirt!" There, I can open an old can of worms.

"And so it seemed that we struck up a conversation just the same. I still met the pretty brunette, turned blonde, girl. In fact, I married said girl." He looked so pleased with himself. I was going to be sick.

"But you didn't come to talk to me because I was me. You were looking for someone else."

"You make a lot of assumptions. I said I prefer brunettes; I never said I wasn't interested in the beautiful blonde girl sitting on the bench. How else would one strike up a conversation with a stranger than to bring up a common thread?"

"I don't know. I can think of a billion ways other than talking about another girl."

"I didn't know much about the camp, art, or tigers." He looked so innocent.

"Were you waiting for the brunette to show up?"

"No, you were already there, and you haven't changed your hair color since, have you? See?"

"So you want to take me back to the zoo?"

"Yes, and I want to make things right. Just you and me and lunch on a bench near the tigers with the pretty brunette girl I heard people talking about. Is it a date?" He rested his forehead against mine. My heart skipped a beat.

"A thousand yeses." I grabbed hold of his hand.

"That is the same answer you gave me twenty years ago when I asked you to be my wife. Would you still give me that answer today if I asked again?"

"Asked me what?" I knew what he was talking about. I just wanted to hear him say it. I had been in a happier mood lately; my size 14 clothes were too big and I was back in the 12's!

". . . To be my wife?"

One thing he was always good at—pushing my buttons. "I would still give you a thousand yeses, plus one thousand more. I did promise you forever."

"Forever is a long time."

"Forever isn't long enough." I couldn't have thought of a more romantic present then a day at the zoo with Horace.

Freedom from Paper Piles: Organizing Your Paperwork

Despite the dawning of the digital age, we have more paperwork than ever. We hold onto letters, magazines, junk mail, newspaper articles, and computer printouts as if life could not go on without them. And once we've filled our file cabinets, storage boxes, bags, and horizontal surfaces with all that paper, we are simply too overwhelmed to process it all. If only there were sprays to make those paper monsters go away!

Whether you are drowning in paper clutter, waste too much time looking for papers you need, or just want to simplify your paperwork management processes, you can use the **5-W Process** to gain control over the paper monsters in your home. Ask and answer the following questions:

***WHY* do I need to keep this paper?** Asking *why* is always the first step in any de-cluttering process. There are only two reasons to keep any paper: to *act* on it now, or to *find* it later. Your first step, then, will be to decide whether the paper requires immediate action on your part or you simply want to be able to find it sometime in the future. (Of course, if you neither need to act on it now nor find it in the future, you should toss it!)

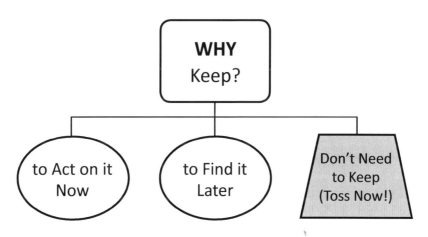

***WHO* cares whether or not I keep this paper?** In some cases we are encouraged, or even required, to keep certain papers. For example, it would cost you time and money to replace your driver's license, or your tax-supporting documents if you're audited. In other instances, we mistakenly believe we must keep papers that really serve us no purpose. Much paper clutter results from people being afraid to discard papers because they *might need them someday*. The fact is there are very few people who actually care whether or not you keep certain papers. Below is a chart of the most common people who care and the documents they want you to keep.

WHO Cares? What They Want You to Keep

The IRS	• Documents that support your tax returns (listed separately below) • Copies of previous returns
Insurance Companies	• Auto, homeowners, and liability policies (date new policies received) • Current disability, medical, life, fire, long term care and personal property insurance policies • Proof of continuous health insurance statements
Creditors/ Vendors	• Account number, mailing address, phone, and website from each company from whom you receive a bill • Agreements and notices of changes • Mortgage and loan discharge statements
Contractors	• Copies of signed contracts • Receipts and warranties for major purchases • Investment purchases and sale confirmations
You and Your Family	• Medical records (listed separately below) • School report cards and standardized test results • Current activities and information • Employment documents • Vital documents (listed separately below) • Some memorabilia
Nobody	• Don't need to keep (Toss Now!)

Documents that Support Your Tax Return:

- ✓ Pay stubs
- ✓ Bank statements
- ✓ Records of dividends received
- ✓ Social Security income statements
- ✓ Pension income statements
- ✓ Rental income records
- ✓ Business income records
- ✓ Records of alimony received
- ✓ Records of other taxable income
- ✓ Charitable donation receipts
- ✓ Medical, dental, and vision expense receipts
- ✓ Prescription medicine receipts
- ✓ Health insurance explanation of benefit statements
- ✓ Statements or receipts for taxes paid (including real estate tax, estimated tax payments, and personal property tax)
- ✓ Mortgage interest statements
- ✓ Business expense records
- ✓ Records of other tax-deductible expenses (including interest payments, unreimbursed job expenses, tax preparation fees, and safe deposit box rental fees)
- ✓ Annual tax forms and statements (W-2s, 1099s, etc.)

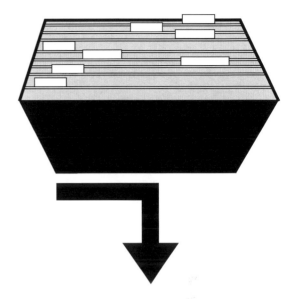

How to Organize:

Set up an expanding folder for the current year and each of the past 6 years. Label the tabs using the relevant categories from the chart on the left. Keep the current year's folder in a convenient location and add papers to it throughout the year as you receive them. Store the 6 prior years' folders in deep storage—just in case you are audited.

Medical Records:

- ✓ Doctor and hospital reports and notes (organized by provider or event)
- ✓ Test results (by test type)
- ✓ Immunization records
- ✓ Rx drug information sheets
- ✓ Manuals for portable medical equipment

How to Organize:

Set up one 3-ring binder with dividers for each family member. Label the divider tabs using the relevant categories from the chart on the left. Insert papers by section in reverse chronological order. Keep the binders in a convenient location. Add new medical records as you receive them.

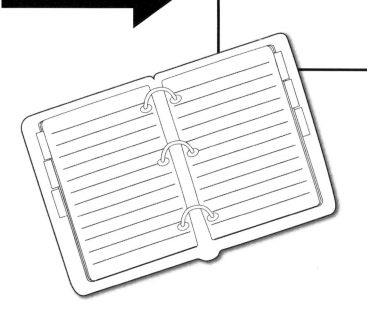

Vital Documents:

- ✓ Adoption papers
- ✓ Automobile titles
- ✓ Birth certificates
- ✓ Citizenship papers
- ✓ Copies of wills—Keep original in your attorney's will safe or with your executor. Keep a copy, not the original, in a safe deposit box.
- ✓ List of credit card accounts and numbers
- ✓ Death certificates
- ✓ Deeds and mortgage papers
- ✓ Divorce decrees
- ✓ Family historical information and negatives of important photos
- ✓ Funeral and burial arrangements
- ✓ Household inventory and appraisal—keep as long as is current; update periodically
- ✓ Important contracts
- ✓ Investment certificates
- ✓ Leases
- ✓ Letter of Last Instructions—Keep original at home; keep a copy in safe deposit box
- ✓ Life insurance policies
- ✓ List of bank account numbers
- ✓ List of insurance policy names and numbers
- ✓ List of internet usernames and passwords
- ✓ Living Wills—Keep original at home; keep a copy in safe deposit box; give a copy to your doctor
- ✓ Marriage certificate
- ✓ Military records
- ✓ Passports
- ✓ Patents, copyrights, and trademarks
- ✓ Powers of attorney—Keep original at home; keep a copy in safe deposit box
- ✓ Retirement plan information
- ✓ Social Security records
- ✓ Stock and bond certificates

How to Organize:

Except for the items noted, the originals of these documents should be stored in your safe deposit box or in a home safe. Keep copies at home in a file marked Permanent Records/Vital Documents, and note the location of the originals on the inside of the file folders.

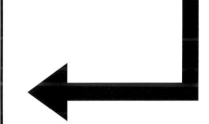

***WHAT* is the next action I need to do with this paper?** When you come across a paper that requires you to take action, rather than filing or tossing it, ask yourself what the NEXT ACTION is that you need to take. For example, if the paper is a bill, the next action will likely be to PAY the bill. On the other hand, if you think there's an error on the bill, your next action would probably be to CALL the billing department. Sorting papers by next action needed allows you to save time by grouping like activities together, such as making phone calls at the same time and paying bills at the same time. The following flowchart lists examples of possible NEXT ACTIONS; feel free to create your own list using action words that are meaningful to you.

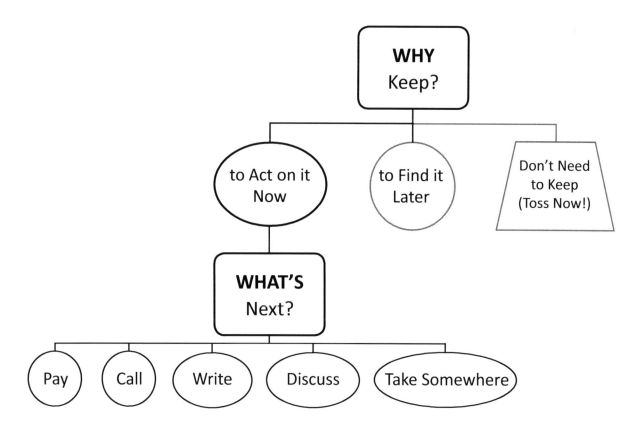

***WHEN* will I need to find this paper?** Your answer to this question will help you answer the next question. Papers, like everything else in your home, should be stored as close to their place of use as possible. Additionally, papers and things you use most frequently should be stored in the most easily accessible locations. The reverse is also true: papers and things you hardly ever use can be stored in less accessible places—that is, assuming you really need or want to keep them at all.

***WHERE* is the best place to store this paper?** Your papers requiring immediate action (pay, call, write, discuss, take somewhere) need to remain visible. Do not file them in a file drawer or file cabinet. You need to set up a system you trust to *temporarily* hold these papers requiring action until your scheduled time to act on them. (Remember how Mary blocked out Sunday evenings to work on her household paperwork?) The system that temporarily holds your action items is called an **Action Box** and has the following characteristics:

- It is open on top (so you can easily see inside as a visual reminder to take action);

- It is big enough to hold folders in an upright position but small enough to fit on top of your desk;

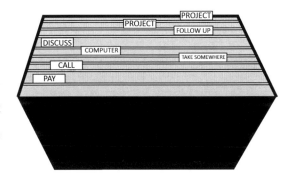

- It contains folders labeled with your Next Actions (pay, call, write, discuss, take somewhere, current projects, and any other action folders that are meaningful to you); and

- The folders in the Action Box look different than the file folders in your file cabinet. If you use manila or green hanging file folders in your file cabinet, consider using colored or transparent folders in your Action Box.

WHERE to store your papers that **require** immediate action:

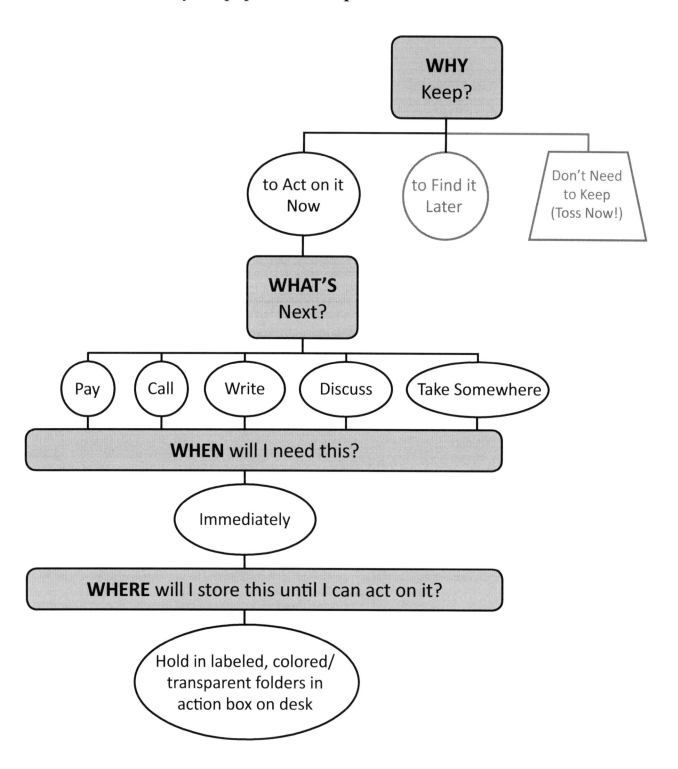

WHERE to store your papers that *do not* **require** immediate action:

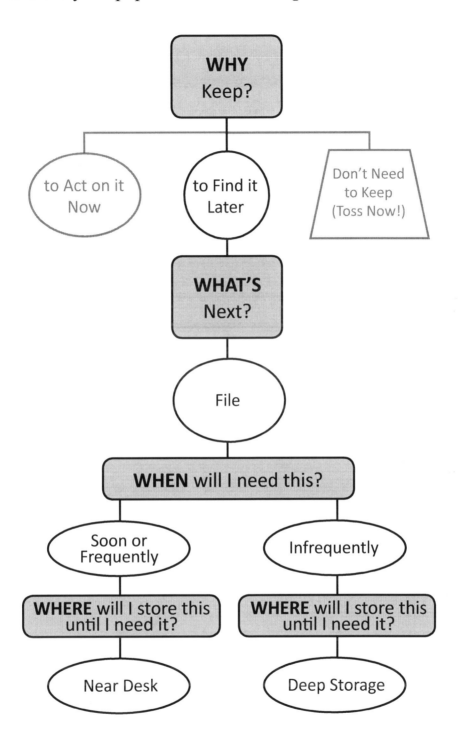

Got Electronic Clutter?

You can use the same process described above to purge and organize your electronic documents. Instead of creating paper file folders, simply create electronic file folders and drag or scan your documents into them. Delete any unneeded electronic documents. The same rules apply to both paper and electronic documents: If you don't need to act on them now or retrieve them later, you don't need to keep them!

What to Shred vs. What to Recycle

We have worked with many people who are reluctant to recycle *any papers containing identifying information.* They accumulate piles and bags of papers to be shredded—someday. But that elusive day when they actually have time to sit and shred all those papers, well, it never comes.

What *must* you shred? The short answer—any documents containing information that someone could use *to try to impersonate you,* including:

- Your signature
- Account numbers (all)
- Social Security numbers
- Date of birth
- Maiden name
- Mother's maiden name
- Medical records
- Legal documents
- Financial information (all)
- Credit card applications
- Online usernames
- Passwords and PINs
- Expired credit cards/ID cards
- Resumes
- Report cards and transcripts
- Employment records

Most of us can easily understand why it is important to shred papers containing our Social Security number, but some of us feel the need to shred even more documents. Should we shred the address labels on catalogs, magazines, and junk mail? Many fear the loss of privacy, not just identity theft, and that causes hesitation when deciding what to toss in the recycle bin. If you are worried about someone finding out your name and address, you may be surprised to learn that your private information is not as private as you had hoped. With a quick internet search, it is quite easy to find someone's name and address. You should feel confident recycling mail that contains your name and address—you don't have to shred it first.

MARY, ACCIDENTS HAPPEN
July 15th, 2000

The flowers on the dining room table were never so fresh and fragrant. They were indeed special—Horace and I grew them. We decided to work in the garden this summer. It suited my artistic desires and gave both of us some needed exercise. In addition, our home never looked so inviting. I had ordered a few books, notice I said just a few, on perennial gardens so we could plant once and reap the rewards of our labors year after year. Horace liked to map out a plan of where to plant everything. That has always been his way. For me, I liked to go with the flow trying out different color combinations and flower types. Things just had a way of taking the right shape and design. Our yard was turning into a work of art.

There was nothing more relaxing then sitting on the back patio at night, lemonade in hand, and enjoying the newly landscaped patio. In a way, Horace and I didn't need to spend money on a fancy vacation; we created our own little hideaway in the backyard.

Mother Nature is simply magnificent when you think about it. She has quite the organizational task each year. She purges all the old flowers and leaves each year and then produces new ones that look just the same as the year before. You have to appreciate the timing and planning of Mother Nature. She is good.

Yes, the summer was progressing nicely, until Horace phoned me one Sunday in the early afternoon. He had gone golfing. If I remember correctly, the conversation went something like this . . .

"Mary, it's Horace. Everything is fine. I just want to let you know that John drove me to the hospital."

As I was relaxing with Moxie in the garden, I remember saying, "Okay, what happened?"

"My back hurt."

"You still haven't answered why you are at the hospital. You've never been to the hospital because of your back before." I tried to remain calm.

"I don't know exactly what happened. I was at the ninth hole ready to tee-off and my back just gave out. I was on the ground." His voice trailed-off and was quiet for a moment. "The pain was pretty severe. They've given me some type of shot to help with the pain, but they want me to follow-up with my doctor. They think I have a herniated disc and they are recommending I take it easy for the next few months and look into physical therapy. I think between golf, tango lessons, and gardening I've worn myself out. I feel like an old man."

So, I went and got Horace from the emergency room. He followed his doctor's orders and went to physical therapy for his herniated disc. His office set him up to work from home, and we now have a lounge chair on the back patio so he can enjoy the garden from a reclined position.

"Mary, I feel so old. I don't know why I can't do what I used to." Glums sat on his lap mirroring his discontent.

I hadn't realized Horace was feeling so down. He was always the voice of reason, and now I had to step-up to the plate.

"Horace, you aren't old. You'll heal and you'll learn to listen to your body when it tells you it can't do something." I smiled at him. Glums looked so cute curled up in his lap. Honestly, I think the cats enjoyed the lounge chair more than Horace.

"The mail is piling up again. There are bills from the doctors and hospital that I haven't felt like opening. Mary, I know I usually take care of the finances, but I could really use your help. I was thinking, what if I had a heart attack out on the golf course and I was gone? You need to know how to take care of things in case I'm not here."

"Horace, you aren't going anywhere." He was so silly.

"Mary, accidents happen. That is why people have life insurance. In fact, I was thinking we might want to make an appointment with our insurance company to see if we have enough coverage." He looked sincere as he peeked at me from behind his glasses. His eyebrows were now a salt and pepper mix and matched the color of the hair over his ears.

"Okay, if it will make you feel better why don't we make an appointment to talk with the insurance company, and I will pay the bills and take care of the finances until you are feeling better." I gave him a smile. I had no idea how I was going to pull that off, but I would surely try.

"Do you know how?" Again, he was so sincere and concerned.

"No, but you don't need the added stress of that responsibility right now so I'll make it work. We're a team. Perhaps you can go over what needs to be done and I can copy what you do?" I made a gesture like I was scribbling notes on a pad of paper.

He smiled. "When?"

"Let me guess, you were thinking right now?"

"It would make me feel much better to know the bills were getting paid, Mary."

So, I managed to get Horace comfortable in the office and we went to work. The pile of mail was ready to topple, but we held hands. We moved all of the junk mail to the recycle bin and he explained how he had been calling to cancel most of the unwanted mail and catalogs we received. (I was curious why the mailbox wasn't as full!) We took our time and sorted one piece of mail at a time. Some papers we filed and others he put in the *Bills to Pay* folder, in the action box on his desk. I wouldn't miss that one!

After we put all the bills in the *Bills to Pay* folder, he told me he paid bills every-other Friday morning. I marked it on the calendar so I would remember to keep the appointment with myself. I really didn't want to incur fees or late notices again, and I didn't want the papers to pile back up.

Horace had already set-up automatic bill payments for the gas, electric, and phone. Really, all we had to do was record the regular monthly expenses in the checkbook—the bank did all the work. Horace had set Nadine's college tuition payment as a recurring monthly payment. Each month, the college deducted a portion from the checkbook, again, one less thing we had to remember to pay.

Since we had so many doctor bills, Horace and I created an action folder for medical expenses and a separate action folder for the insurance company's EOB (Explanation of Benefit) forms. We made sure, before we paid any medical bills, that we could match the bill to the correct EOB form from the insurance company. We didn't want to pay a medical bill that hadn't first been processed by the insurance company, and we didn't want to pay any bill twice. Horace told me to file the paid medical bills and their matching EOBs in the tax file. As we needed to keep track of our medical expenses for tax purposes, his filing suggestion was genius!

Horace also refreshed my memory on how to balance the checkbook. It was something I hadn't done in a long time, but he had been keeping up with it each month so it wasn't hard for me to pickup and follow. Horace gave me these four easy steps to follow to master the art of checkbook balancing:

1. Match the entries in our check register with the entries on the bank statement. Put a check mark next to each matching entry in both the register and on the bank statement.

2. Look over the bank statement to find any unchecked withdrawals or deposits. (Sometimes Horace and I forget to write them in our check register, especially those ATM cash withdrawals!) Add any transactions we missed into the check register then check them off.

3. Look over the check register for any unchecked deposits or withdrawals. Those transactions are usually more recent and weren't cleared by the bank at the time the bank statement was prepared. Circle those transactions in the check register. They will probably show up on next month's statement.

4. Make sure our checkbook balance matches the amount the bank says we have! The bank makes this pretty easy by putting a reconciliation chart on the back of the bank statement. I just need to do a little math:

    Ending balance on the bank statement
    + Deposits we've made that weren't on the bank statement
    − Withdrawals we've made that weren't on the bank statement
    = Our current checkbook balance

Horace told me to make sure this was done each month as it was part of our *reality check*—the reality of what we really have in the bank and what we spend. Besides, we needed to make sure enough money was in the checkbook each month to cover the automatic bill payments.

Horace's secretary, Alexis, had shown Horace how to make a file index so he could find any file at work when he needed it. It listed each file name, alphabetically, and the location of the file in his office. He kept a copy in the front of his file drawer and she held a spare—just in case. Apparently Horace loses things, too! He suggested we make a file index for our home so we both knew where to find files when we needed them. He also recommended we let Nadine know where the file index was in case she should ever need to find something. *What if we both weren't here?*

"Mary, I think I need to go back down and lie on my chair." Horace looked exhausted. "I may have to leave the gardening to you for awhile, but I eventually want to put my dance and golf shoes back on." He got up out of the chair gingerly. "You know there is one other thing we should make a list of."

"You and all of your lists . . . ." He was so serious.

"It wouldn't hurt to have an index of all of our assets and debts. We don't need to keep track of figures, just the names of the institutions where our bank accounts and loans are, along with the account numbers. If anything were to happen . . . ."

I cut him off. "Nadine and I would be just fine. You concentrate on getting better, Horace. You have taken care of things for us; now let us take care of you."

Freedom from the Daily Mail: Organizing Your Bill-Paying Process

A bill-paying system is a specific set of steps taken to process and pay your bills on a regularly-scheduled basis. Whether you pay your bills electronically, by phone, or by paper check, use the *MESS* formula to organize how you pay your bills.

*M*ove Out the Excess

Eliminate junk mail, unwanted solicitations for money, and unwanted e-mails. Reducing the amount of physical or visual clutter will help you focus on the important items, like unpaid bills, that remain.

*E*xamine One Category at a Time

When you open your mail or e-mail, sort it into categories based on the type of action you need to take on each item. Your bills need to be sorted into a paper or electronic folder of their own, because the action you need to take on them is to *pay* them. It is critical that you separate bills to be paid from other paperwork or electronic documents.

*S*et Rules

After you've gathered your bills into a *Bills to Pay* folder, store the folder in your action box on your desk. Does this step make you worry that you might forget about your bills? Most people rely on visual cues to stay organized, so it's important that you keep your action box visible. Don't hide it in a drawer or cabinet. You will need ready access to the *Bills to Pay* folder to add new bills as they arrive, so carve out a prominent spot for your action box on your desk. For electronic bills, create a *Bills to Pay* folder on your computer desktop. Commit to keeping your *Bills to Pay* folder in the same place all the time.

Systematize

Create a bill-paying schedule. The easiest thing to do is to schedule bill-paying time to coincide with payday. (It's always helpful to have money in the bank when you go to pay your bills!) But don't just rely on your memory! Schedule bill-paying time on your calendar as an appointment with yourself, or schedule it as a recurring appointment if you use an electronic planning system.

When bill-paying day arrives, sit down at your desk and pay your bills. If you cannot or choose not to pay all of the outstanding bills at one time, write the bill's due date on the outside of the envelope and put it back in your *Bills to Pay* folder to help you prioritize future payments.

Store a supply of envelopes, stamps, return address labels, checks, and pens near your *Bills to Pay* folder so you won't waste precious bill-paying time searching for them.

Do you ever wish your bills would pay themselves? In some cases, you can make that happen! With some simple up-front work on your part, you can reduce the number of checks you need to write each month. Here are three electronic bill-paying options to consider.

1. Set up automatic deductions (debits) with each of your service providers

Most people have a number of recurring bills—some monthly, some quarterly, and some semi-annually or annually. These bills are usually for routine or non-discretionary purchases that are more-or-less essential to our lives, but may be different amounts in each billing cycle. Some examples of these recurring expenses include:

- ✓ Electricity, heating oil, & natural gas
- ✓ Telephone (landline & cell)
- ✓ Internet
- ✓ Water & sewer
- ✓ Automobile insurance
- ✓ Homeowner's or renter's insurance
- ✓ Cable or satellite TV
- ✓ Credit card payments

To set up automatic deductions for bills, call the customer service phone number or visit the biller's website. You will need to give each biller your checking account routing number (the first 9-digit number in the bottom left-hand corner of your checks) and your checking account number. In some cases, you will need to send a voided check to the biller. It usually takes 1 or 2 billing cycles for automatic deductions to begin. During that time, you'll need to double-check any bills you receive to see whether or not you need to send in a payment.

2. Switch to online bill-paying through your bank

If you don't want to set up automatic payment of your bills, or if you simply want more control over when your bills are paid but still want to save yourself some time, then online bill-paying through your bank's website will be a great tool for you. There are many benefits to online bill-paying.

- You get to decide the date on which the bill will be paid.

- You can pay anyone through online banking, individuals or companies, as long as you know their mailing address.

- You can easily track your prior payments to a particular person or company.

- Most banks guarantee that the payee will receive your payment by the designated date, and will even cover late charges if the payment arrives late.

- Online bill-paying saves you money—no more postage stamps and check re-order charges.

- It's safe.

- It's almost always a free service offered by your bank.

- If you're not already enrolled in online banking with your bank, you will need to set that up before you can start paying bills online. Go to your bank's website to enroll, or contact the bank's customer service line for instructions.

> *Automatic deductions are not appropriate for everyone. If you don't carry a sufficient cushion of funds in your checking account to cover automatic deductions, your bank could charge you fees. If you receive a regular paycheck, and know you will always have a sufficient amount of cash in your checking account, however, automatic payments will be a huge time saver for you.*

3. Set up recurring online payments through your bank

Some of your bills are for the same amount each billing cycle. These bills are perfect candidates for you to schedule as recurring online payments through your bank. Examples of bills with recurring amounts include:

- ✓ Rent or mortgage payments
- ✓ Alimony & child support payments
- ✓ Homeowner's association payments
- ✓ Subscriptions/payments
- ✓ Loan payments (car, student, personal)
- ✓ Storage unit rent
- ✓ Home security system monitoring
- ✓ Life insurance premiums

Rather than take the time to enter these recurring payments every time they are due, you can schedule recurring payments through your bank's online bill-paying service. When the payment amount changes or you no longer need to pay the bill, you can easily adjust the payment amount online.

Summary of your bill-paying options:

Payment Method	Best for	Be Aware
Paper checks	• People who prefer to write checks • Occasional bills • Paying for in-store purchases	Make sure you don't run out of checks.
Automatic deductions	• Regular payments when payment amounts differ each billing cycle	Continue to monitor bills to ensure accuracy of deductions.
Online bill-paying through your bank	• People who want to maintain more control over when their bills are paid	Make sure you schedule payments in sufficient time so the bank can process them before they are due.
Recurring payments through online bill-paying via your bank	• Recurring payments to billers who charge the same amount each cycle	Remember to adjust the online payment amount if the billing amount changes.
Payment by phone or wire transfer	• True emergencies • When you have neglected to follow your bill-paying system and a bill payment would otherwise arrive late	Both methods take longer to execute than other payment methods, and wire transfers cost you money.

Organizing Your Medical Bills

Mary and Horace were fortunate. Horace's injuries were not life-threatening; he would fully recover. And they had health insurance that covered most of Horace's medical bills. Nevertheless, the medical paperwork that accompanied Horace's mishap piled up quickly. Mary had to sort through bills and statements from dozens of doctors she had never heard of as well as bills from the emergency room and hospital. Not unlike many people in her situation, Mary was overwhelmed. The shock of a loved one's injury, the responsibility of their care, and the time required to make sense of the mountains of medical bills and statements would make many of us want to crawl under the covers.

Mary used the *MESS* formula to organize their medical bills and statements, and you can, too.

*M*ove out items that don't belong

Medical bills, unlike bills for electricity or rent, need some special attention before you pay them. To give them your full attention, create separate action folders just for *Medical Bills to Pay* and *Explanation of Benefit (EOB) Statements to Review* (the statements you receive from your medical insurance company). You will store these action folders in an Action Box on your desk. (Refer to page 71 for how to set up an Action Box.)

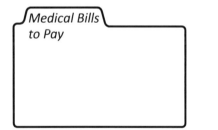
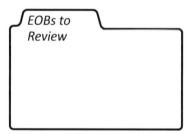

*E*xamine one category of items at a time

If you have a lot of medical bills and EOBs to process it will be helpful for you to spend some time organizing the contents of each folder before you proceed with the steps below. Arrange the bills in your *Medical Bills to Pay* folder in chronological order by *date of service*. Arrange the EOBs

> *Why organize the contents of the* **Medical Bills to Pay** *and* **EOBs to Review** *folders differently? Some insurance companies combine claims for different dates of service on the same EOB, which makes it difficult to organize these EOBs by date of service.*

in your *EOBs to Review* folder in chronological order by ***statement date***. Highlight service and statement dates so they are easier to find again.

Set rules

What you do with each of your medical bills before you pay it will depend on how you answer these questions:

Is the bill legitimate? Did you or a member of your household actually receive services from the listed healthcare provider, and does the date of service listed coincide with the date you received services? Doctors' offices, hospitals, and their billing services make mistakes. Make sure the bill is yours before you pay it. If something is wrong, call the billing department phone number listed on the bill ***immediately***. Keep detailed notes of when you call, with whom you spoke (get a name), and what was said.

> *If your provider does not submit claims for their patients, you will need to obtain a claim form from your insurance company. Check their website for a downloadable form and submit it yourself.*

Are you required to pay the bill? Just because you have checked to be certain the bill is legitimate does not mean you're required to write a check. If you have medical insurance, you will want to make sure the insurance has covered its part of the bill before you pay your portion. Skipping this step could result in a duplicate payment of all, or a portion, of the bill. Before you write a check, examine each bill and EOB carefully to find the answers to these questions:

- ***Was this bill submitted to your insurance company by your healthcare provider?*** Some providers will submit a claim to your medical insurance before they send you a bill. The bill will show whether or not the provider submitted a claim. If there is no mention of an insurance submission on the bill, contact your provider's billing department to make sure they have your correct insurance information and ask them to submit the claim.

- ***Has the insurance company covered its portion of the bill?*** If the provider submitted an insurance claim, the bill will show you how much the insurance company has paid (or applied to your annual deductible amount). Open your *EOBs to Review* folder and locate the EOB for that particular bill. The EOB will tell you how much of the bill the insurance company paid, and how much, if anything, is your responsibility.

- ***Did you look at the Patient Responsibility column on your EOB to determine the exact amount you need to pay?*** Even if the provider's bill shows a remaining balance due after your insurance company has made a payment, the provider may have agreed to accept the insurance company's payment as payment in full. You may owe nothing.

After you have completed these steps, you can pay any remaining portion of your bill with confidence.

Systematize how you put things away

File the paid medical bill and its corresponding EOB in your tax folder. Why your tax folder and not your medical file? Because your tax folder is where you'll need to find these documents next. If you claim medical expenses as a deduction on your tax return, you will need to total those expenses when preparing your tax return next year. Medical *records* get filed in your medical file. Medical *bills* that have been paid, along with their corresponding EOBs, get filed in your tax folder.

Return an unpaid medical bill to the *Medical Bills to Pay* action folder if your insurance company has not yet responded, or if you have a dispute with the bill. Be sure to keep notes of any actions you have taken, including phone calls and the date you submitted an insurance claim for the bill. Revisit the bill during your next bill-paying session.

The following diagrams illustrate the above process of reviewing and paying your medical bills. (Please note: One flow diagram is for *submitted bills*, the other *for bills that have yet to be submitted to your insurance company.*)

Medical Bills That Have Been Submitted to Insurance

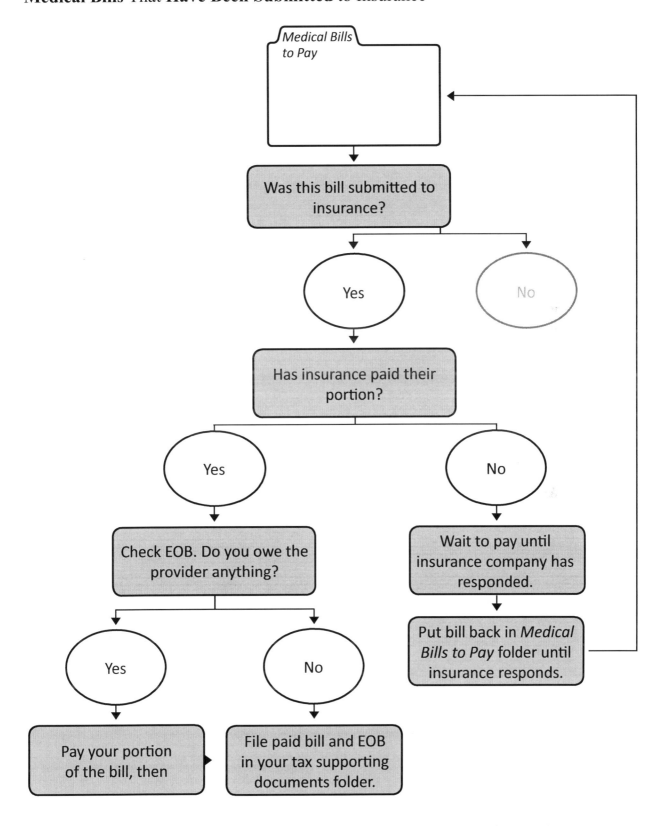

Medical Bills That Have Not Been Submitted to Insurance

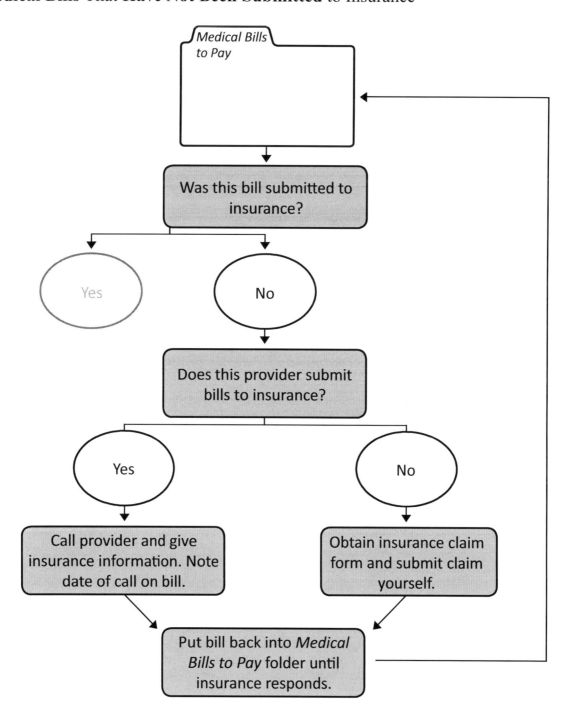

WHAT IF...
October 5th, 2000

My favorite black, patent-leather pumps were covered in mud—I didn't even give a damn. Life always seems to have a way of bending you to its will, of making you realize it is time to make a needed change, or of whispering in your ear that our time on earth is fragile.

Nadine's eyes were glossed over with tears. Horace was trying to keep both Nadine and me sheltered from the rain with his golf umbrella, but the wind was picking-up and causing the rain to attack us at an angle. Everyone at the cemetery was soaked.

Susan had been a close friend of Nadine's since kindergarten. They grew up together, learned how to drive together, and graduated together. Susan's mother, Kelly, was not just a second mother to Nadine—she was my friend. Cancer is neither prejudiced nor impartial. It doesn't interview its potential hosts and leave the good-hearted alone. Cancer is blind. Kelly didn't deserve to lose her fight with cancer; she was one of the ones who should have survived.

Horace and I had a quiet dinner alone at home. We had stopped to pick up some Chinese carry-out, but we were both so upset that we just stared at our food. Nadine was staying the night at Susan's. The house was eerily quiet. Even Horace's grandfather clock seemed to chime a song of mourning. I hadn't seen any of the cats since we got home.

Horace broke the silence. "Mary, I know we made a list of our assets and debts this summer, but when I met with the insurance company to update our life insurance coverage they asked if we had a will. They also asked if we had a home inventory to supply them should we need to file a claim with our homeowner's insurance."

"Horace, I don't know if we should talk about this right now." I was already so upset.

"Actually Mary, now is the perfect time. What if you and I were to die in a car crash tomorrow, or God forbid, what if the house burned down! No one plans for these things to happen, but they do."

"Horace, I can't think about Nadine being an orphan, not even at 18."

"That is why we need a will, Mary. It will make things easier on Nadine if anything were to happen to us. We should also set up a power of attorney for each other and health care directives in case one of us becomes too ill to make our own decisions. The death of a loved one is a horrible thing, but those left behind have to keep on living. Nadine already knows where all of our financial and personal documents are. She even has an index to find what she needs. I'd like to think of a will as a gift to Nadine—it shows that we care about her and her future."

Horace was right. We needed to meet with a lawyer. "Make an appointment with the lawyer, Horace. This is something we should have done a long time ago."

Horace reached across the table and held my hand. "Are you okay?"

"Time heals all wounds." I tried to put on a smile. "Kelly was a good friend, Horace. I will miss her."

"So will I Mary." Horace squeezed my hand. "So will I."

Freedom from Worry: Organizing Your Estate Planning

Remember the old saying: The only two certainties in life are death and taxes? Most of us don't *forget* to file our tax returns because the federal and state governments are kind enough to give us deadlines, as well as the incentive to file on-time to avoid interest and penalties.

Unfortunately, however, there is no such deadline (pun intended) for getting our legal affairs in order. It's an uncomfortable subject for many of us. After all, we feel young and healthy. We're careful drivers. We won't have to worry about *those things* for many years. Right? Maybe yes, but maybe no. The fact is that none of us know when we will die or become incapacitated and unable to make decisions for ourselves. Therefore, we have to be prepared—and organized. Although your personal situation may require additional estate planning, *everyone* (including *you*) needs to have these three legal documents in place.

Legal Documents You Need to Have

1. Last Will and Testament (or Revocable Living Trust)

If you have one, is it up-to-date? Does it have the appropriate level of federal and state tax planning based on current laws? Have you named a guardian for your minor children and the appropriate person to serve as your personal representative? Are your assets titled appropriately?

2. Power of Attorney

A power of attorney is a document that lets you name another person to make financial decisions for you. It should be *durable*, meaning that it will be exercisable even if you were to become disabled or incapacitated.

3. Advance Health Care Directive

Your medical directive lets you name someone to make medical decisions for you if you cannot make them for yourself. It also states how you want your health care handled if you are in a life-threatening situation. If you have been certified as incapable of making an informed decision regarding your medical treatment, and you don't have a health care directive, the law will specify who can make those decisions for you. Does your medical directive reflect your current wishes?

It took Horace's health scare and Kelly's death to prompt Mary and Horace to organize and update their legal documents. Don't wait for something like that to happen to your family before you take care of these matters. Life can change in an instant.

Schedule a meeting with your estates and trusts attorney if any of the following situations apply to you.

- You do not have the above mentioned legal documents in place.
- Any of your estate planning documents is more than 3-5 years old.
- Your marital status has changed.
- You have a new child/children.
- Your children have become adults.
- You have changed your state of residence.
- Your assets have had a major change in value.
- You need to appoint a new executor or personal representative.
- You are approaching retirement.
- You are concerned that your legal documents aren't up-to-date.

Where to Store Your Legal Documents

Even good, up-to-date legal documents are worthless if no one can find them when the time comes. Be sure to store your legal documents safely, and inform your executor, children's guardian, and attorney-in-fact of where to find them.

Will: Store the original, signed document in your attorney's will safe. In some jurisdictions you can store your will at the courthouse. Give an executed copy to your personal representative, and keep a copy at home with your other vital documents. ***DO NOT*** store your original will in your safe deposit box. Your safe deposit box will be sealed upon your death. Unless someone else is listed as an owner of the box along with you, no one will be able to access your will.

Power of Attorney: Give the original, signed document to your *attorney-in-fact* (the person you have named to make financial decisions for you). Keep a copy with your other vital documents.

Advance Health Care Directive: Give the original, signed document to the person you have authorized to make your medical decisions. Give a copy to your doctor(s) for your medical chart, and keep a copy with your other vital documents.

> *If you have a power of attorney that is more than 3-5 years old you should know that it might not be accepted by everyone. Is your power of attorney up-to-date?*

What My Family Needs to Know

If something ever happens to me . . . Just in case you ever need to know where my things are . . . If I die . . . We've all heard, and perhaps even said, phrases such as these at one time or another. They are euphemisms for a subject that we don't like to talk about, but know that we should talk about: our own death or the death of a loved one. Nevertheless, we *must* plan for it, organize for it, and talk about it because there is no *if* when it comes to death.

Consider another possibility that could happen at any time: You could become physically or mentally incapacitated by an accident. If such an unexpected event were to happen to you, would your family easily be able to locate the information they need to maintain your household? Would they be able to locate your medical history to communicate with your doctors?

What *does* your family need to know? They need to know your personal, legal, medical, and financial information ***and*** where to find it. Create a *What My Family Needs to Know* booklet to help your loved ones attend to the administrative matters required upon your death or incapacity.

How to create your *What My Family Needs to Know* booklet

1. From the information you have already gathered, compiled, and organized, create a booklet of your personal, legal, medical, and financial information. You will find worksheets for each of these information categories below. You can also find these worksheets at www.absolutely-organized.com. Photocopy a set of the blank worksheets for each member of your family.

2. Fill in all applicable information on each worksheet. If any item on the worksheets is not applicable to you, write N/A in the box next to the item so your family members will know the item doesn't exist and they won't waste time looking for it.

3. As you complete your worksheets, you may come across important matters you need to address. For example, when completing the My Personal Information worksheet, the *Preferred Funeral Home* and *Preferred Place of Burial* items might remind you that you've been thinking about pre-planning your funeral.

4. When items on the worksheets remind you of a task or project you need to work on, you need to capture that thought. Immediately schedule a specific time in your calendar to work on that task.

Choose a file name that makes sense to you so you can find the document again. Be sure to include the date in your file name. When you update any information, update the file name with the latest date so you'll always know which information is most current.

When your worksheets are complete, remember the job is not quite finished. You spent time creating these documents for your loved ones—now you need to save, secure, and share them.

SAVE: If you completed your worksheets by hand, consider scanning them into your computer and saving them in the cloud or on a flash drive. If the paper copy gets lost or damaged, you can print a new copy.

SECURE: Your worksheets contain sensitive information. Password-protect the file you have saved on your computer. Create a booklet of the printed worksheets by placing them in a thin 3-ring binder. Store the booklet and the flash drive with your other vital documents.

SHARE: Give your loved ones a paper copy of your booklet and/or a copy of it on a flash drive. If you share the document electronically, don't forget to share the password, too!

MY PERSONAL INFORMATION	
Full legal name, including maiden name	
Social Security #	
Date of birth	
City and state of birth	
Country of birth (if outside U.S.)	
Contact Information	
Address (physical)	
Address (mailing)	
Home phone	
Work phone	
Cell phone	
Fax	
E-mail address 1	
E-mail address 2	
Marital Status	
Marital status	
Spouse's full name, including maiden name	
Date of marriage	
City and state of marriage	
Former spouse's full name, including maiden name	
Date of marriage to former spouse	
Date of divorce & name of court where divorce was granted	

Family	
Mother's full name, including maiden name	
Father's full name	
Next of kin	
Address	
Phone #	
Secondary next of kin	
Address	
Phone #	
Secondary next of kin	
Address	
Phone #	
Secondary next of kin	
Address	
Phone #	
Secondary next of kin	
Address	
Phone #	
Secondary next of kin	
Address	
Phone #	
Secondary next of kin	
Address	
Phone #	

Important People	
Clergy person/place of worship	
Personal representative/trustee	
Children's legal guardian	
Lawyer	
Accountant	
Financial advisor	
Banker	
Insurance agent	
Insurance agent	
Insurance agent	
Veterinarian	
Preferred funeral home	
Preferred place of burial	
Other relatives	
Trusted friend or neighbor	
Out-of-area contact person	
Business, School, & Social	
Current employer or school	
Former schools/colleges & graduation years	
Fraternity/sorority	
Social, business, & association memberships (list individually)	
Business Licenses	

Military Service	
Branch of service	
Dates of service	
Rank	
Service number	
Date of discharge	
Type of discharge	
Service-connected disabilities (%)	
Other Important Data	
Home voice mail retrieval code	
Cell phone voice mail retrieval code	
Home alarm code	
Computer access password	
E-mail address(es)	
E-mail username(s) & password(s)	
Social media username(s) & password(s)	

MY LEGAL INFORMATION	(INCLUDE LOCATION OF ORIGINAL DOCUMENTS)
BIRTH CERTIFICATE: DOB, city & state, certificate #	
ADOPTION CERTIFICATE: date of adoption, city & state	
MARRIAGE CERTIFICATE: date of marriage, city & state	
ANNULMENT CERTIFICATE: date of annulment, city & state	
DIVORCE CERTIFICATE: date of divorce, city & state	
NATURALIZATION PAPERS: date of citizenship, certificate #	
MILITARY DISCHARGE PAPERS: date of discharge, certificate #	
PASSPORT: date of issue, passport #	
DRIVER'S LICENSE: date of issue, driver's license #	
DEATH CERTIFICATES OF CLOSE RELATIVES: location of certificates	
FINANCIAL POWER OF ATTORNEY: date created, name & contact info for agent	
MEDICAL POWER OF ATTORNEY: date created, name & contact info for agent	
ADVANCE DIRECTIVES: names of people who have copies	
LIVING WILL: names of people who have copies	
ORGAN DONOR? where your desire is documented	
WILL: location of original, date created, any codicils, attorney's contact info, executor's contact info	
TRUST(S): date created, attorney's contact info, trustees' contact info	
LETTER(S) OF INSTRUCTIONS: location, names of recipients	
FUNERAL & BURIAL cemetery name, address, & lot numbers, deed to cemetery lot, preferred recipient(s) of memorial gifts, desires for funeral ceremony, location of prepaid funeral services document	

MY MEDICAL INFORMATION				
Providers	**Name & Address**	**Phone**	**Fax**	**Acct. #**
Primary Care Physician				
Specialist _____				
Specialist _____				
Specialist _____				
Specialist _____				
Specialist _____				
Specialist _____				
Specialist _____				
Specialist _____				
Specialist _____				
Dentist				
Pharmacist				
Health Insurance – Primary				
Health Insurance – Secondary				
Health Insurance – Rx Drugs				
Health Insurance – Dental				
Health Insurance – Vision				
Medicare				
Medicare Part D – Rx Drugs				
Medicaid				
Long-Term Care Insurance				
Prescription Drugs (Name)	**Purpose of Drug**	**Dosage (mg)**	**Time(s) when taken**	

OTC Drugs/Supplements (Name)	Purpose	Dosage (mg)	Time(s) when taken	
Allergies - Medicines	**Possible reactions**		**Treatment(s)**	
Allergies – Food	**Possible reactions**		**Treatment(s)**	
Allergies – Other	**Possible reactions**		**Treatment(s)**	
Prior Hospitalizations	**Reason**	**Hospital**	**Date(s)**	
Prior Surgeries				
Immunizations - Childhood		**Date**	**Date**	**Date**
	Hepatitis B			
	Rotavirus			

Immunizations - Childhood		Date	Date	Date
	DTaP			
	Hib			
	Pneumococcal			
	Polio			
	Influenza			
	MMR			
	Varicella			
	Hepatitis A			
	Meningococcal			
	Other			
	Other			
Immunizations – Teen		Date	Date	Date
	Tdap			
	HPV			
	Meningococcal			
	Pneumococcal			
	Hepatitis A			
	Hepatitis B			
	Polio			
	MMR			
	Varicella			
	Other			
	Other			
Immunizations – Adult		Date	Date	Date
	HPV			
	Varicella			
	Zoster			
	MMR			
	Influenza			
	Pneumococcal			
	Hepatitis A			
	Hepatitis B			
	Meningococcal			
	Other			
	Other			

MY ASSETS					
Name & Address of Institution	Account Number	Contact Person	Phone	E-mail	Website, Username, & Password
Checking & Debit Card Accounts					
Savings Accounts					
Homes/ Real Estate					
Vehicles					
Certificates of Deposit					
Stocks					
Bonds					
Mutual Funds					
Retirement/ Pension Plans					
Life Insurance Policies					

Other Assets	Account Number	Contact Person	Address/Location	Phone	E-mail
Put a check next to each type of asset you own, then enter the data for each asset.					
Airplanes					
Alimony Receivable					
Antiques					
Artwork					
Boats					
Bonuses Receivable					
Businesses Owned					
Buy/Sell Agreements					
Cemetery Plots					
Child Care Receivable					
Collections					
Combinations to Locks					
Copyrights					
Deferred Compensation Receivable					
Employer Benefits					
Foreign Income					
Frequent Flyer Miles					
Hidden Cash					
Home Improvement Receipts					
Home Inventory List/Photos/Video					
Items on Loan to Others					

Other Assets	Account Number	Contact Person	Address/Location	Phone	E-mail
Limited Partnerships					
Livestock					
Loan Payments Receivable					
Location & Contents of Storage Units					
Location of Keys					
Mortgages Held					
Notes Held					
Partnerships					
Patents					
Pets					
Real Estate					
Retirement Benefits					
Royalties					
Safe Deposit Boxes & Location of Keys					
Social Security					
Stock Certificates					
Stock Options					
Tax-Related Documents (current year)					
Tax-Related Documents (prior years)					
Treasury Bills					
Valuable Home Furnishings					
Veteran's Benefits					

Other Assets:	Account Number	Contact Person	Address/Location	Phone	E-mail
*					
*					
*					
*					
*					
*					
*					
*					

MY INSURANCE POLICIES						
Put a check next to each type of asset you own, then enter the data for each asset.						
Type of Insurance	Husband	Wife	Child #1	Child #2	Child #3	Child #4
Whole Life						
Term Life						
Travel						
Long Term Care						
Health (Primary)						
Health (Secondary)						
Dental						
Vision						
Homeowner's						
Personal Property						
Renter's						
Automobile						
Business Property						
Business Liability						
Worker's Comp						
Dishonesty Bond						
Other:						

Put a check next to each type of asset you own, then enter the data for each asset.	
Type of Insurance	
Insurance Company Name	
Mailing Address	
Broker's Name	
Broker's Mailing Address	
Broker's Phone	
Broker's Fax	
Broker's E-mail	
Policy Holder's Name	
Policy Number	
Amount of Insurance	
Location of Policy	
Other Information	
Type of Insurance	
Insurance Company Name	
Mailing Address	
Broker's Name	
Broker's Mailing Address	
Broker's Phone	
Broker's Fax	
Broker's E-mail	
Policy Holder's Name	
Policy Number	
Amount of Insurance	
Location of Policy	
Other Information	
Type of Insurance	
Insurance Company Name	
Mailing Address	
Broker's Name	
Broker's Mailing Address	
Broker's Phone	
Broker's Fax	
Broker's E-mail	
Policy Holder's Name	
Policy Number	
Amount of Insurance	
Location of Policy	
Other Information	

MY BILLS	Name of Creditor/ Vendor & Mailing Address	Account Number	Payment Frequency	Phone	Website, Username & Password
Credit Cards:					
Loans:					
Car Loan 2					
Mortgage Payment					
Home Equity Credit Line					
Household Bills:					
Cable TV					
Childcare					
Church/ Synagogue Pledges					
Debts/ Obligations					
Electricity					
Gas					
Insurance:					
Whole Life Insurance					
Term Life Insurance					
Travel Insurance					
Long Term Care Insurance					
Health Insurance					

HOUSEHOLD BILLS	Name & Address	Account Number	Payment Frequency	Phone	Website, Username & Password
Insurance:					
Dental Insurance					
Vision Insurance					
Homeowner's Insurance					
Personal Property Insurance					
Renter's Insurance					
Automobile Insurance					
Business Property Insurance					
Business Liability Insurance					
Worker's Comp Insurance					
Dishonesty Bond					
Other Insurance:					
Internet					
Laundry/Dry Cleaning					
Lawn Service					
Membership Dues:					
Pest Control					
Pet Sitting					
Pledges Made					
Rent					
Satellite TV					
Snow Removal					

	Name & Address	Account Number	Payment Frequency	Phone	Website, Username & Password
Subscriptions:					
Tax Payments:					
Telephone - cellular					
Telephone - landline					
Telephone - long distance					
Tuition					
Other:					
*					
*					

MAKING A LIST AND CHECKING IT TWICE
November 15th, 2000

The season of gift-giving was approaching fast. How did I know? Well, besides the frozen turkeys that were stocked at the grocery store, there were also holiday catalogs and charity requests for giving in our mailbox. Most of the organizations I had never even heard of—but I love looking at catalogs. Those bad little monsters are always in my mailbox!

Horace was calling a lot of the companies we received catalogs from to stop the mailings, but apparently our name was still out there, somewhere. And as mail and sorting paper are two of my least favorite things to do in this world, I was shocked to see how many holiday catalog companies knew who I was. Then I remembered back to last year. I had come a long way. I am *The Little Engine That Could.*

I found an old cardboard box and put it in the garage—right by the door. After I gathered the mail each day I would do a quick sort on my walk up to the door, and into the box the holiday catalogs went. I didn't even bring them into the house. I'd let Horace know the catalogs were there and when he had the time he could call some of the companies and tell them to save some trees. This was a DO NOT BUY zone.

Horace and I had done a good job of sticking to the budget, so the holiday-gift-giving money we had set aside was there to be spent. We were still trying to work on paying off the credit card bills. It was a slow process, but each month our debt was shrinking. We had actual results of our labors and it worked as a great motivating tool. I might even be able to get my new kitchen updates next year!

Horace had asked me to make a list for gift-giving this year. I mapped out little columns with names of family and friends. I also included a few art charities I wanted to support, and of course, I couldn't forget to donate to the zoo! Now that the weather was getting colder there were not as many visitors at the zoo. Now, more than ever, the tigers needed some help.

When I finished with the gift-giving list I gave it to Horace. As usual, he was calm when he looked it over. "Nadine needs a new computer, a new phone, AND all of these other things? Mary, I love Nadine too, but we are going to blow our gift-giving budget on Nadine alone."

He was my reality check. Reality wasn't always fun.

"And I don't need to be on the list. I thought we agreed no gifts." Horace was so sincere.

"Yes, but it's Christmas." I batted my eyes at him. It didn't work.

"I thought Santa was working to bring us a new kitchen and pay-off our credit card bills? Remember all those items from Christmases past?"

"Yes, I want that, too. By the way, while you are editing the gift-giving list I should tell you I started a box of holiday catalogs in the garage. I refuse to bring any of them into the house. I guess they ignored your requests of DO NOT SEND for the holidays?" He smiled as if to note he knew I was changing the subject.

"No, they are probably catalogs that companies only send yearly to entice people during the holidays. Glad you created a box, Mary. I will take it with me to work and make a few calls at lunch. I was reading that companies sell your name and address to other companies for advertising. I will start to specify that we don't want our name sold and that we don't want any mail from them or their partners."

"There are a lot of charity requests in the box, too. What do you want to do with those?"

"I guess the same thing, Mary. I'll call some of them, but I think you had a good idea of listing the places you wanted to donate to as part of our gift-giving list. It is much easier to keep track of who we are donating to when we just write one check to each organization at the end of the year. We know what we have to give, and we can file a receipt right in the tax file so we know where it is."

Horace loved his organized files. I was doing my best to stick to the paper plan we set-up. It was becoming an easier process, but I needed a gentle reminder now and then. Paper was not my friend.

"I do think we can weed this list down a little more, Mary. And instead of giving gifts that take up space, maybe we can think about giving gifts people can consume. Most people surely don't need anything else, but a gift card to dine out or a nice bottle of wine is always nice to have."

"I guess I won't be shopping on the television then." I tried not to sound too disappointed.

"Have you been?!"

"No!" I was hoping to watch a little over the holidays though. Unfortunately, they don't sell gift cards on television. "But old habits are hard to break."

"You've been doing a good job, Mary. I shouldn't have implied . . . ."

I gave Horace a hug. I know what he meant—he didn't have to explain. After all, there were some golf and electronic gadget catalogs in the garage box and I knew I wasn't the only one who was resisting the urge to spend.

Horace and I had agreed only to spend $600 on holiday gifts this year. So, we sat down and planned how we would distribute the $600 among the people and charities on our gift list. The holidays wouldn't be easy, but we were a team. Here is our final chart:

Holiday Gift and Charity Donation Plan

Name	Maximum Gift Value	Total Remaining Gift Budget: $ 600
Donation to Zoo	-100	500
Donation to Art Museum	-100	400
Nadine	-300	100
Horace	No gifts - saving for new kitchen	100
Mary	No gifts - saving for new kitchen	100
Alexis	-75	25
Neighborhood Gift Swap	-25	0

Freedom from Guilt: Organizing Your Gift Giving

The holiday season is the perfect time to remember to share our blessings with others in need.

Plan and track your charitable giving

File any new receipts for charitable donations in your tax folder. The U.S. Internal Revenue Service requires you to obtain a receipt from the charitable organization as proof of a cash/material contribution if you itemize deductions. For current IRS requirements, go to *www.irs.gov*.

Many charities send multiple requests throughout the year. You may or may not want to contribute more than once. Look in the *charity* section of the current year's tax folder to find receipts from charities to which you've already donated.

Create a simple spreadsheet containing the date of donation, charity name, and amount of donation given. Total the amount column. File the spreadsheet in your tax folder for reference when you prepare your income tax returns.

Make your gift-giving list, but check it twice

List-making is a kind of therapy for many, especially when they are under a time crunch at the end of the year. We love to make holiday lists: gift lists, food shopping lists, holiday card lists, to-do lists, and lists for Santa Claus.

But simply making lists is not enough. The first draft of a list tends to be a brain dump—a mish-mash of everything and everyone we can think of. Before you hit the stores or the internet during the holiday season, take a second look at your lists. Consider these questions:

1. Who can you eliminate from your list? Do you have to give gifts to all your adult relatives? They might be relieved to hear a suggestion to draw names within the family and exchange gifts with one person only.

2. Can you give a gift of service instead of spending money? Perhaps you and your friends or family members could spend time together volunteering at a charitable organization this year, rather than exchanging gifts.

3. Who on your gift list will appreciate your time more than your money? Your grandmother doesn't need another sweater. Why not give her what she really wants: time spent with you. Give her a gift certificate for a day of help sorting through photos or clearing the attic.

4. Can you give consumable gifts instead of more stuff? Do the people on your list really need more stuff? Many adults have more clothes and household items than they know what to do with. Some children get so many toys they don't even know what they have. If you must buy something, consider things that can be consumed, such as food, gifts cards, and movie tickets.

Try using Mary's gift-giving list. Below is a blank copy for your use. You may end up finding your wallet doesn't need a big workout this holiday season.

Holiday Gift and Charity Donation Plan

Name	Maximum Gift Value	Total Remaining Gift Budget: $ _____

READY FOR REFLECTIONS
December 31ˢᵗ, 2000

Dorothy, from *The Wizard of Oz*, had the means throughout her entire trip in Oz to go home—her ruby-red slippers. Once she realized how much she wanted to go home, when she was *ready* for change, she learned how to use those ruby-red slippers to travel home. Dorothy didn't miss her house; she missed her home.

I would call my house a home. My home has all the things I love in it: Nadine, Horace, Moxie, Glums, and Fiasco. And home wouldn't truly be home without the beat of Horace's grandfather clock. Many of the things in my home that I didn't need or want are gone. All of the monsters are fading. I will no longer make excuses—I am the best monster spray. I plan to continue exterminating my home.

As another New Year arrives it is a good time for reflection. I think resolutions are best made during the year, but the year's end is a good moment to look at where you've been, where you are going, and where you want to be. I am in a much better place than I was last year. I have made new plans with Horace as to where *we* want to go. I have adjusted my journey so that I will continue to find myself in a place I truly want to be.

Horace and I made a return trip to the zoo for a holiday fundraising brunch. While there, we saw a sign posted for summer intern applications. Nadine is thinking about working there this summer, and I have already advised her to watch out for any business interns hanging around the tiger cage. But I'll be watching. In fact, Horace will be watching, too. We both enlisted to serve as volunteers at the zoo. It had sort of felt like home, being back where we met, watching the tigers, and enjoying the zoo. It isn't a huge commitment, just twice a month, but as I said we can keep an eye on the human tigers that are around this summer. It was a brilliant match. I was ready.

I think *ready* is a powerful word. Not just for Dorothy, but for all of us. Dorothy had to travel to a far-off land to realize what she missed most, and along the way she helped others, and herself, gain knowledge, heart, and courage. Nice things to have when walking the road of change, those roads less traveled. And when we are ready we always seem to find just what we need and the help to get there. For instance, I can't count how many times I have given tours as a docent at the museum. Then, the other week, I had a small group of children come through the president's room where replicas of presidential busts are housed. As the children made themselves busy, I found myself standing next to the bust of Abraham Lincoln. On the nearby walls, the museum has presidential quotations posted. I had read some of them through the years, but the one behind Lincoln's bust was a new one to me, or at least one I never noticed. It read, "And in the end, it's not the years in your life that count. It's the life in your years." Well said, Abe. Well said.

Celebrating Your Freedom from Disorganization

As Mary discovered, the last week of the year is a time for reflection. Questions you will want to ask yourself include: How closely did I stick to my spending plan? Am I spending more time on the people, things, and activities that are most important to me? What changes do I need to make next year to align my behavior with my priorities? Take the time to skim through the chapters of this book and note any topics you still need to address next year. Use the goals and action plan provided in the *Planning Your Journey to Freedom from Disorganization* chapter to set a plan for the upcoming year and seek the help of others for direction, encouragement, and assistance when you need it.

Always celebrate your organizational successes. If the rooms in your home function as intended, if your finances are in order, and if your vital documents are organized so that you or someone else can find them in an emergency, then you have made significant progress toward living a more organized life. Congratulations! If you're not as far along in your journey as you had hoped you would be, don't feel down. Sometimes life gets in the way of our best intentions. The good news is that we have the opportunity to begin again. Resolve to build on your past successes in the New Year.

Having an organized life is not a once-and-done event. It is a lifelong process that requires practice and maintenance. And, as Mary learned, it is often best achieved with the help and ongoing support of others.

Mary's desire to lead a more organized life was not unique, but her journey was. We hope her story and the *Now It's Your Turn* portions of this book have provided you with the inspiration and creative avenues you can use as you seek organizational freedom. As Mary noted in her comparison to Dorothy in the *Wizard of Oz*, you need to be *ready* to make a change. We are all wearing a pair of ruby-red slippers; we just need to know how to use them. It won't always be easy, but like Mary you have the heart, and like Dorothy you now have the courage and the knowledge to walk a new path—to take a new journey. Our wish is that one day *you* will create your own success story entitled, *My Journey to an Organized Life*.

Katherine Trezise, CPO, CPO-CD, MBA, is the president of Absolutely Organized. She is a past president of the Institute for Challenging Disorganization. Katherine has traveled as far as Canada and Japan speaking on the topic of organizing. She has shared her expertise with *The Wall Street Journal*, *Bloomberg Business Week*, *Style* magazine, and WMAR television. She was a contributing writer for *The ICD Guide to Collaborating with Professional Organizers* and Jerry Baker's *Can the Clutter.* Katherine has a bachelor's degree in psychology and a master's degree in business administration.

Jennifer Power is a professional writer and former professional organizer. In addition to writing a weekly blog on organization, Jennifer has been published in *The Chronical*, a publication of the Institute for Challenging Disorganization. She has appeared on WBFF FOX 45 News Baltimore as a guest commentator on organizing. Jennifer has a bachelor's degree in business administration and a master's degree in professional writing.

Made in the USA
Middletown, DE
22 October 2015